NO LACK OF COURAGE

Operation Medusa, Afghanistan

COLONEL BERND HORN

FOREWORD BY
General (Retired) R.J. Hillier

D1324389

DUNDURN PRESS
TORONTO

Editor: Cheryl Hawley
Design: Jennifer Scott
Printer: Webcom

Library and Archives Canada Cataloguing in Publication

Horn, Bernd, 1959-
   No lack of courage : Operation Medusa, Afghanistan / by Bernd Horn ; foreword by R.J. Hillier.

Includes index.
Also issued in electronic format.
ISBN 978-1-55488-766-8

1. Operation Medusa, Afghanistan, 2006. 2. Afghan War, 2001- --Regimental histories--Canada. 3. Canada--Armed Forces--Afghanistan. 4. Courage--Afghanistan--Case studies. I. Title.

DS371.4123.O655H67 2010   958.104'7   C2010-902421-4

1   2   3   4   5   14   13   12   11   10

Conseil des Arts du Canada / Canada Council for the Arts

Canada

ONTARIO ARTS COUNCIL
CONSEIL DES ARTS DE L'ONTARIO

We acknowledge the support of the **Canada Council for the Arts** and the **Ontario Arts Council** for our publishing program. We also acknowledge the financial support of the **Government of Canada** through the **Canada Book Fund** and **The Association for the Export of Canadian Books**, and the **Government of Ontario** through the **Ontario Book Publishers Tax Credit** program, and the **Ontario Media Development Corporation**.

Printed and bound in Canada.
www.dundurn.com

Dundurn Press
3 Church Street, Suite 500
Toronto, Ontario, Canada
M5E 1M2

Gazelle Book Services Limited
White Cross Mills
High Town, Lancaster, England
LA1 4XS

Dundurn Press
2250 Military Road
Tonawanda, NY
U.S.A. 14150

CONTENTS

Foreword   9

Introduction   11

Chapter One — "Exporting Stability": Canada and Afghanistan   15

Chapter Two — A Growing Storm   25

Chapter Three — Genesis of an Operation   37

Chapter Four — Opening Salvos   49

Chapter Five — Chaos at the White Schoolhouse   61

Chapter Six — Tragedy at Dawn   79

Chapter Seven — Payback   93

Chapter Eight — Declaring Victory   111

Chapter Nine — The Reality of the Long War   121

Epilogue   145

Notes   151

Acknowledgements   193

Glossary of Abbreviations   195

Index   199

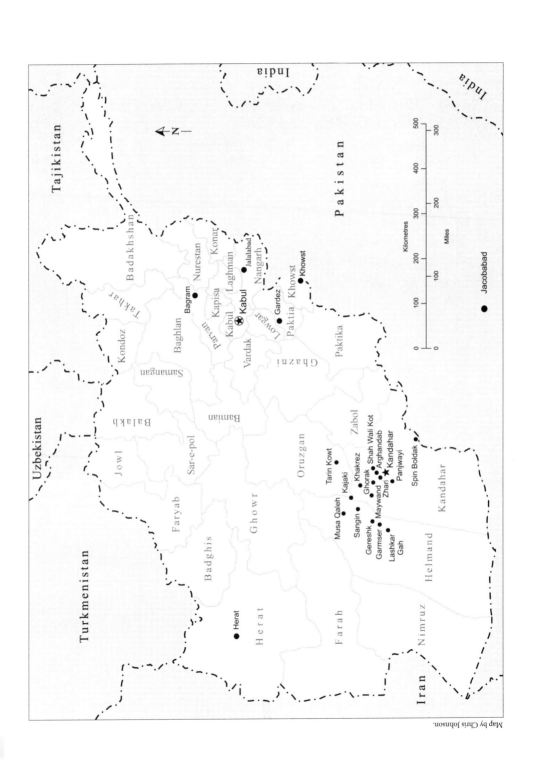

FOREWORD

I AM DELIGHTED to have been given the opportunity to write the foreword for *No Lack of Courage: Operation Medusa, Afghanistan*. As an officer in the Canadian Forces for over 35 years, I had the privilege of serving with many of the finest men and women Canada has to offer. Significantly, as the chief of the Defence Staff, I had the honour of commanding our country's sons and daughters while our nation was at war. Throughout that period I was struck by the courage and tenacity of our service personnel and especially their families. Heroic individuals who, despite the pain of loss or grievous injury, maintained a stoic disposition because of their love of country and belief in the cause for which they or their loved ones fought. Their courage constantly buoyed my own spirit through those tragic periods when we suffered casualties.

But more importantly, their strength reinforced my belief in our own warrior spirit. For much of my career the Canadian Forces was described as a peacekeeping military and our soldiers, sailors, and airmen as peacekeepers. Too often our proud military legacy as war-fighters was conveniently ignored in preference of a more benign descriptor as humanitarians and "Blue Berets." Seemingly lost was the belief that our Canadian Forces were actually capable of combat operations.

Afghanistan changed that perception. Everyone, from our fellow Canadians to our Allies and coalition partners to even our enemies, has been reminded of the courage and tenacity of the Canadian soldier. And no event was more seminal in passing on that message than Operation Medusa.

During those two weeks in September 2006, in the hot, dusty killing fields of Panjwayi, in Kandahar Province, Afghanistan, Canadian soldiers, like their forefathers before them, fought desperate and savage battles to defeat a vicious and brutal enemy intent on imposing their will on others.

The cost was high. On that terrible Labour Day weekend in 2006, one of the engaged sub-units, Charles Company of the 1st Battalion, The Royal Canadian Regiment Battle Group, lost their company commander, a company sergeant-major, one out of three platoon commanders, all three platoon warrant officers (one wounded, two killed), five of nine section commanders, and all of their sections' second-in-command master-corporals. In total, they suffered five killed and more than 40 wounded in a 48-hour period. But it is important to note that those who survived stepped up. A young sergeant promoted to that rank less than a year earlier became the company sergeant-major. Young master-corporals became platoon commanders and platoon second-in-commands. Equally remarkable, young soldiers became section commanders and they carried on the operation and the fight against the Taliban that gave NATO such an incredible boost. After all, political and military decision makers in Afghanistan and NATO all publicly stated that Operation Medusa, in essence NATO's first actual battle, was key to the very survival of Afghanistan, if not the NATO alliance itself.

And our troops were successful. Fighting a savage enemy in some of the harshest conditions and terrain any Canadian soldier has ever had to endure, they fought in close-quarter combat for days on end and overcame a determined and cunning enemy. In the end, Operation Medusa is a true Canadian epic. *No Lack of Courage* is an amazing account of those tragic yet inspiring days, when Canadians demonstrated the justly earned reputation as fierce warriors. Told in the words of those who were actually there, this book vividly captures an important piece of Canadian military history and should be read by everyone.

General (Retired) R.J. Hillier

Introduction

THE OPPRESSIVE HEAT and relative calm of the Afghan afternoon betrayed the overpowering undercurrent of tension permeating the area surrounding the non-descript, white schoolhouse complex nestled in the Panjwayi District of Kandahar Province. Hidden away in bunkers and fortified buildings was a group of fanatical Taliban fighters, tightening up the slack on their triggers as they nervously eyed the approaching Canadian vehicles. Simultaneously, the soldiers from "C" Company (Coy), 1st Battalion, The Royal Canadian Regiment Battle Group (1 RCR BG), rolled their vehicles slowly toward the suspected enemy position. In a split second the hot, relatively quiet countryside erupted in a fusillade of noise, explosions, and death. The fight was on.

That event, which became known as Operation Medusa, was a major offensive conducted by the International Security Assistance Force (ISAF) with assistance from the Afghan National Army (ANA), from 1–17 September 2006. Their objective was to establish government control over an area of Kandahar Province centered on the district of Panjwayi, approximately 30 kilometres from Kandahar City, the birthplace and heartland of the Taliban. The region was undeniably an enemy stronghold. The North Atlantic Treaty Organization's (NATO) intent, under whose auspices ISAF was operating, was to destroy or capture the insurgents who had dug-in to fight. Initially the campaign design followed a phased approach of engaging the local leaders diplomatically, to attempt to minimize the level of death and destruction in the immediate area, and then to apply superior and precise combat power as required. By 2 September 2006 it was apparent that combat was inevitable. The brunt of that combat fell to the Canadians.

The road to Operation Medusa was a long one. It began almost five years before on the morning of 11 September 2001 (9/11). At the time, no one could have predicted that the world was about to change. As nations were beginning to come to grips with the instability of the post-Cold War era, a global upsurge in terrorist attacks failed to cause a spike in concern among Western nations. After all, terrorism was a timeless tactic of the weak.[1]

However, the world did change on 9/11. The attack on the twin towers of the World Trade Center, which was as symbolic as it was destructive, struck at the very core of Western values in a way that the world had never experienced. Moreover, it was an attack against Americans on U.S. soil. Not since the infamous attack on Pearl Harbor, on 7 December 1941, had the U.S. suffered casualties due to a foreign hostile act on its homeland.

Not surprisingly, the response was immediate and all-consuming. In retaliation, then-American President George W. Bush declared a global war on terrorism. His first target was the Taliban regime in Afghanistan, accused of harbouring and abetting the terrorist, Osama bin Laden, who was deemed responsible for the attack on American soil. Bush subsequently launched Operation Enduring Freedom (OEF), designed to topple the Taliban and capture or destroy bin Laden and his fellow al Qaeda senior leaders and fighters.

The Europeans, albeit reluctantly, responded in support of their American ally. The reality was that they had little choice. For over half a century the Americans stood on guard at great expense to protect Europe under the NATO alliance. With the assault against the Americans, the Europeans had to live up to the NATO mantra: an attack on one member is tantamount to an attack against all members of the alliance.

The Canadian response was also immediate, if somewhat slow to actually galvanize. Ships were deployed within weeks, special operations forces were on the ground by the end of December 2001, and a light infantry BG was deployed to Kandahar Airfield in February 2002. All were deployed to assist their American counterparts in operations that supported OEF.

Accordingly, the Canadian decision to support the Americans in Afghanistan seemed simple enough, as did Canada's continued contributions to the region. Prime Minister Jean Chrétien's decision to deploy Canadian Forces (CF) personnel and equipment to Afghanistan as part of OEF in 2001–2002 was linked to Canada's commitment to NATO's solidarity and to fighting international terrorism as authorized by United Nations Security Council Resolution 1368.[2] Chrétien decided to return troops to Afghanistan in August 2003, after a brief one-year hiatus, to assist the newly established NATO ISAF mission in Kabul. Two years later, in August 2005, his successor, Prime Minister Paul Martin, approved the redeployment of troops from Kabul in the north to the more volatile and dangerous Kandahar Province in the south as part of ISAF's expansion throughout Afghanistan. Subsequently, Canada assumed command of the Provincial Reconstruction Team (PRT) for the area, as well as responsibility for an infantry BG that was tasked with providing security in the region.

By the spring/summer of 2005, Canadians were heavily engaged in combat with the Taliban. That level of commitment, particularly the loss of soldiers in heavy fighting, earned Canada the respect of its coalition partners. It also secured Canada's position as a major player in Afghanistan. At no time was that role more evident than in the summer and early fall of 2006, when Canadian troops fought pitched battles in the Taliban heartland of Pashmul in Kandahar Province to destroy insurgent forces were poised to launch a major attack to capture Kandahar City, thereby threatening the tenuous hold the central Government of Afghanistan (GoA) held over the country.

Operation Medusa, from 1–17 September 2006, represented the climax of that struggle. This epic combat engagement was NATO's first battle in its nearly 60 years of existence. Importantly, it was fought primarily by Canadians. As one senior officer acknowledged after the operation, "we were basically told, you're on your fucking own for while." General Rick Hillier, the chief of the Defence Staff (CDS), later acknowledged, "With the Taliban resurgence, we didn't have the troops on the ground to do the job the way it had to be done." He explained, "Canada was in the middle of a life-and-death firefight in the south, and few in the alliance were willing to step up and help." Hillier lamented, "We were essentially in it by ourselves, with Americans and British troops, and that made me angry."[3]

Certainly, Operation Medusa was a significant Canadian benchmark. It signalled to Canadians and allies that Canada was once again ready to engage its personnel in combat operations. The nation finally put to rest the peacekeeping myth that it had acquired in national and international psyches since the 1950s and once again overtly proved itself as a warfighting nation within the international defence community. In fact, Admiral Mike Mullen, the chairman of the U.S. Joint Chiefs of Staff, had confided to the CDS that the Americans "had written off Canada as a serious player, a contributor, to anything that was going to happen around the world." However, Operation Medusa and the follow-on Canadian efforts in Afghanistan had changed all that. "Now you guys are at the forefront of everything positive," Mullen stated. "You're setting the example for countries in Europe to follow, for other Western countries, for any country around the world to follow, and you guys are doing it. It's absolutely incredible."[4] The high praise was certainly welcome, but it should not have been a revelation. After all, Operation Medusa merely confirmed that there is no lack of courage when it comes to the Canadian soldier.

CHAPTER ONE:

"Exporting Stability": Canada and Afghanistan

THE SKY WAS A clear blue and the leaves were just beginning to change colour. It was another beautiful early fall day in northern Ontario as the commanding officer (CO) of the 1st Battalion, The Royal Canadian Regiment (1 RCR), drove into the training area of Canadian Forces Base (CFB) Petawawa to do a range reconnaissance for an upcoming exercise. As his vehicle meandered deeper into the heavily forested rolling hills his cellphone erupted, shattering the calm stillness of the vehicle.

"Colonel, you have to come back — something's happened, I think it's important that you be here," was the cryptic message passed to the CO. Trusting the judgment of his highly intelligent and perpetually calm operations officer, the CO told his driver to return to base. Upon arrival, he was able to watch the second commercial airliner plough into the south tower of the World Trade Center. The battalion was the immediate reaction unit for Land Forces Central Area (LFCA) and without delay began preparing for whatever mission would follow. Little did the "Royals" in 1 RCR know that the events unfolding in New York on the tragic morning of 11 September 2001 would lead to the killing fields of Panjwayi five years later, and would cost so many of them their lives.

The brazen attack by terrorists who, armed solely with cheap, 99-cent box cutters, hijacked fully fuelled commercial airliners and used them to strike not only the two towers of the World Trade Center in New York, but also the Pentagon in Washington, D.C. A fourth hijacked jetliner heading for Washington, D.C., slammed into the ground in Pennsylvania, short of its objective due to the bravery of its passengers. In total, almost 3,000 people were killed in the attacks.

Not surprisingly, Washington responded quickly to the 9/11 attacks in order to protect the American homeland and U.S. facilities and installations abroad. The Americans suspected that Osama bin Laden and his al Qaeda (AQ) terrorist network were responsible for the attacks. They realized that they would need to strike their antagonists overseas. On 14 September, the American Congress authorized President George W. Bush to "use all necessary and appropriate force against those nations, organizations, or persons [who] planned, authorized, committed, or aided the terrorist attack on September or harboured such organizations or persons."[1]

The Americans also called on their NATO allies for help. NATO's North Atlantic Council met on 12 September to discuss the U.S. request to invoke Article 5 of the North Atlantic Treaty that defines "an armed attack against one or more of the Allies in Europe or North America" as "an attack against them all," and thereby requires each ally to "assist the Party that has been attacked by taking such action as it deems necessary."[2] This was the first time that the Article 5 clause had been invoked.

By 2 October the Americans provided their allies with "clear and compelling evidence" that the AQ had, in fact, been behind the 9/11 attacks. Two days later, NATO Secretary General Lord Robertson announced that the Alliance would take collective actions to assist the United States. As such, it dispatched an Airborne Early Warning component (an aircrew consisting of 22 Canadians, 55 Germans, and 74 Americans) to assist with the campaign against terror, and it deployed elements of its Standing Naval Force to the eastern Mediterranean Sea.[3]

In accordance with Treaty requirements, NATO also notified the UN that it intended to invoke Article 5 under the framework of the United Nations Charter provision affirming the inherent right of member states to individual and collective defence. However, the UN Security Council had already met to address the 9/11 attacks on 12 September and urged all states to work together "to bring to justice the perpetrators, organizers, and sponsors of the attacks." In essence, the UN had already given its approval to NATO on 28 September, when they invoked Chapter VII of the United Nations Charter, which authorized the use of military force.[4]

Then, on 7 October 2001, the United States and the United Kingdom informed the Security Council that they were taking military action in self-defence, specifically that they were undertaking operations to strike at al Qaeda and Taliban terrorist camps and training and military installations in Afghanistan.

Canada reacted quickly as its southern neighbour and its European allies mobilized for war. On 9/11 Canada, in accordance with its obligations under the North American Aerospace Defense (NORAD) treaty, became immediately involved.[5] Moreover, on 7 October, the day the Americans launched Operation Enduring Freedom, Canadian Prime Minister Jean Chrétien announced that Canada, "standing shoulder to shoulder with ... the American people" would deploy sea, land, and air forces to assist the United States.[6] The Standing Committee on National Security and Defence affirmed, "in those early days the Committee saw two good reasons for Canada to play a role in Afghanistan. One was supporting our long-time American ally in a time of need. The second was that any initiative that our Government could take to counter international terrorism, as called upon by the United Nations, had merit."[7]

Shortly after the prime minister's announcement, the deputy chief of the Defence Staff (DCDS) responsible for CF operations, issued his intent for Operation Apollo, the code name given to the CF's support to the American war on terror. On a national level, the strategic aim was to protect Canada, specifically to prevent future attacks on Canada or its allies by eliminating the threat of terrorism. As a result, the government set a number of national objectives:

a. Focus all elements of national, diplomatic, financial, developmental assistance, economic, military intelligence, and law enforcement in order to neutralize the threat posed by terrorists;
b. build the widest possible international coalition against international terrorism including, in particular, the participation of the Islamic world; and
c. make use of all appropriate means to deter and eliminate the support, harbouring, or cooperation of state and non-state actors of terrorists organizations of terrorist organizations.

To ensure that the overarching objectives were achieved, the government also established a set of immediate military objectives that would be undertaken in cooperation with the U.S. and other coalition partners and countries within the region. Those objectives were articulated as:

a. isolating the Taliban regime from all international support;
b. bringing Osama bin Laden and leaders of al Qaeda organization to justice;
c. eliminating the al Qaeda organization as a continuing terrorist threat;
d. taking the appropriate military, diplomatic, and economic action to force the Taliban to cease all support, harbouring, and cooperation with al Qaeda; and
e. immediately addressing the humanitarian needs of the Afghan population.

Mid-term objectives were also articulated. Once again, working in conjunction with its allies, Canada set the reconstruction of Afghanistan as its mid-term objective priority.

By October the Department of National Defence (DND) had earmarked an initial conventional Canadian contribution. It included:

a. a naval task group of two frigates (HMCS *Charlottetown* and HMCS *Halifax*), one destroyer (HMCS *Iroquois*), one replenishment ship (HMCS *Preserver*), and five maritime helicopters as of 10 November 2001;
b. one frigate (HMCS *Vancouver*) (with one maritime helicopter) to augment U.S. Carrier Battle Group (CBG) USS *John C. Stennis*;
c. an airlift task group (ALTG) comprised of three C-130 Hercules and one C-150 Polaris aircraft;
d. a long-range patrol task group (LRPTG) consisting of two CP-140 Aurora patrol aircraft; and
e. a national command element (NCE) located with U.S. Central Command (CENTCOM) headquarters in Tampa, Florida.

The CDS provided a clear mission for the deploying troops. He affirmed that the "CF will contribute to the elimination of the threat of terrorism as a force in international affairs by contributing [Canadian] Joint Task Force South West Asia (CA JTFSWA) to the commander-in-chief (CINC) CENTCOM in support of the U.S.A. led campaign against terrorism in order to protect Canada and its allies from terrorist attacks and prevent future attacks." His intent was to support the international campaign through an initial six month commitment of military forces, the role of the CF being further refined as the coalition military campaign plan evolved and matured.[8]

However, the Americans did not wait for the Canadian commitment to be fully mobilized. They utilized special operations forces (SOF), CIA paramilitary forces, and air power to help the Northern Alliance anti-Taliban coalition to quickly cut through the Taliban forces. Kabul fell to the Northern Alliance on 13 November. Priority then shifted to the south, namely the Taliban heartland of Kandahar. Within 63 days of commencing the offensive the Americans and their Afghan allies captured Kandahar.[9] On 14 November, the day after the fall of Kabul, the UN Security Council once again condemned the Taliban government "for allowing Afghanistan to be used as a base for the export of terrorism by the al-Qaeda network and other terrorist groups and for providing safe haven to Osama bin Laden." More importantly, to fill the imminent power vacuum, the UN created a transitional government that would establish a "multi-ethnic and fully representative" government.[10]

To achieve that goal talks were held in Bonn, Germany, on 27 November 2001. The Bonn Agreement called for an interim authority to be established in Afghanistan on 22 December 2001. This body was to provide leadership for Afghanistan until a representative government could be elected through free and fair elections. To ensure a smooth transition, and to provide security until Afghan National Security Forces could be established, UNSCR 1386 was tabled on 20 December 2001. The newest resolution called for a peacekeeping mission in Afghanistan to develop national security structures, assist in reconstruction, and organize and train future Afghan security forces. It also created the British led International Security Assistance Force (ISAF), which was stationed in Kabul.[11] Canada opted not to join the largely European initiative at that time.

Instead, Canada decided to deploy a light infantry BG based on the 3rd Battalion, Princess Patricia's Canadian Light Infantry (PPCLI), on 1 February 2002, to support American operations in the Kandahar area.[12] Throughout the next six months, in support of the American initiatives to destroy Taliban and al Qaeda forces, members from 3 PPCLI and Canadian SOF conducted combat operations with their American counterparts in the Tergul mountain range in the Shah-i-Kot Valley in Eastern Afghanistan, as well as in the Gardēz area. By late July 2002, Canada redeployed these ground forces back home.

However, Canadian ground participation in Afghanistan quickly resumed. On 12 February 2003, Canada's European allies requested Canadian participation in ISAF. John McCallum, the minister of National Defence (MND) at the time, told the House of Commons: "Canada has been approached by the international community for assistance in maintaining peace and security in Afghanistan for the UN mandated mission in Kabul. Canada is willing to serve with a battle group and a brigade headquarters for a period of one year, starting late this summer."[13] He explained, "The ISAF mission is not only essential for continental security. It is also consistent with Canadians' longstanding commitment to peacekeeping and to providing security for people in distress."[14]

The motive was not completely altruistic. "The best defence for Canada is a good offence," insisted Lieutenant-General Rick Hillier, then the commander of the Canadian Army. Canada, he observed, "must play a significant part in the world to prevent that violence and conflict from coming home."[15] As a result, in July 2003 close to 2,000 Canadian troops were dispatched to Kabul as part of Operation Athena, to assist the NATO ISAF mission, which was tasked with providing security in the Kabul area and reinforcing the Afghan Transitional Authority.[16]

Over five successive six-month rotations, Canadian troops conducted foot patrols and surveillance tasks that established a presence and capability within the ISAF area of responsibility. Those tasks also generated intelligence and situational awareness. Canadian soldiers also assisted and facilitated the rebuilding of the democratic process in Afghanistan.[17]

Operation Athena officially ended on 18 October 2005, with the withdrawal of the remaining Canadian sub-unit, the reconnaissance squadron from the Kabul area.[18] But Canada was not leaving Afghanistan. Rather, she was redefining her contribution as part of Stage 3 ISAF expansion into Afghanistan. Canada took responsibility for a Provincial Reconstruction Team (PRT) in the turbulent and insurgent rich Kandahar Province. Canada assumed command of the PRT in August 2005.[19]

The Americans created the PRT construct in November 2002, as part of OEF. It became a critical component of the U.S. efforts to stabilize Afghanistan. PRTs were conceived as a way to integrate diplomats, development officials, military assets, and police officers to address the causes of instability, namely poor governance, weak institutions, insurgency, regional warlords, and poverty.[20]

The 350-strong Canadian PRT copied this multidisciplinary focus that stressed development as well as security. It became a multi-departmental effort, employing personnel from the DND, Foreign Affairs, and International Trade Canada (DFAIT), the Canadian International Development Agency (CIDA), The Royal Canadian Mounted Police (RCMP), and other Canadian police forces. Its mission is to help extend the authority of the Afghanistan government in Kandahar Province by promoting local stability and security, improving local governance structures, and engaging in reconstruction activities. Specifically, the PRT is designed to:

1. promote the extension of the Afghan central and provincial government;
2. implement development and reconstruction programs;
3. assist in stabilizing the local security environment; and
4. support security sector reform. [21]

The adoption of the PRT and the move of the Canadian expeditionary force from Kabul to Kandahar was a deliberate decision. General Rick Hillier, then the CDS, put the Afghan deployment in context. "We must export stability to places like Afghanistan," he explained, "otherwise we will import the instability that results from a lack of action."[22]

Spurred by recent events, he pronounced:

> The impending operations are risky but necessary in light of last week's bombings in the British public-transit system. The London attack actually tells us once more: we can't let up. These are detestable murderers and scumbags. I'll tell you that right up front. They detest our freedoms, they detest our society, they detest our liberties.[23]

Gordon O'Connor, who was appointed minister of National Defence a year later, remarked, "We can't allow the Taliban to return to their former prominence to take over Afghanistan and resume their regime of terror and tyranny; to flaunt their disregard for human rights; to punish and terrorize their own people; to murder innocents; to harbour those who would threaten us and our families at home and abroad."[24] He went on to state, albeit rather melodramatically, that "it's naïve of us to think that Canada is not a pathway to get to America and that Canada would not be the next objective."[25]

The net output of the Canadian commitment was the deployment of an infantry BG of approximately 1,000 soldiers to work with the American forces to conduct stabilization and combat operations throughout Kandahar Province as of February 2006. The American forces were still operating under the framework of OEF and the introduction of the Canadian BG became an integral component of the transition from the American OEF framework to the ISAF Stage 3 transition of NATO control of coalition forces in Afghanistan.[26] This new evolution of the mission was called Operation Archer.

The continuing commitment to Afghanistan was not surprising. "Canadians have never shirked from their responsibility to help those in need, nor has Canada ever failed to take operational leadership when it was necessary to do so," extolled the Standing Committee of National Defence. "Difficult challenges will not deter our national will.

Our military history is the story of Canadians going abroad to fight in the national interest of Canada and on behalf of others who could not defend themselves."[27]

The governmental rationale for the Canadian military commitment to Afghanistan was succinctly articulated:

a. to protect the national security interests of Canada by helping to ensure that Afghanistan will not, once again, become a haven for international terrorists;

b. at the invitation of the democratically elected government of the Islamic Republic of Afghanistan, to help provide a secure environment in which the rule of law, human rights and economic prosperity can grow; and

c. to support our allies and other international friends in the UN, NATO and G-8 by providing leadership in one of the most difficult operational areas.[28]

In the end, the rationale was as much about others as it was ourselves. Former Canadian ambassador to Afghanistan, Chris Alexander, stated, "Our objective isn't to simply invest well-equipped forces under strong leadership into the eye of the storm that is Kandahar. It's to support a transition from 25 years of war to long-lasting peace."[29] Prime Minister Stephen Harper explained, "As 9/11 showed, if we abandon our fellow human beings to lives of poverty, brutality and ignorance in today's global village their misery will eventually and inevitably become ours."[30]

Undeniably, Canada's continued engagement in Afghanistan helps create the conditions for longer-term reconstruction. Canadian Forces operations in Afghanistan have always been conducted with the consent and at the request of the Afghan government. The aims of the CF in Kandahar Province were also clearly thought out. First and foremost the Canadian intention was "to provide the people of Afghanistan with the hope for a brighter future by establishing the security necessary to promote development and an environment that is conducive to the improvement of Afghan life." In addition, the CF was to conduct operations in support of the ANSF, strengthen and enhance Afghan governance capacity, and to help extend the authority of the Government of Afghanistan throughout the southern regions of the country. Finally, the CF effort was to support the larger Canadian integrated whole-of-government team to facilitate the delivery of programs and projects that support the economic recovery and rehabilitation of Afghanistan, as well as assisting in addressing humanitarian needs of Afghans by supporting Canadian governmental organizations and NGOs whose efforts meet Canada's objectives.[31]

The overall effort was in keeping with what a Senate report noted was a long-standing Canadian value. It stated, "Canadians have generally recognized the need to be willing to send troops abroad to defend Canada's interests and values, as well as play the kind of role that any mature country must play in promoting international stability."[32]

And so, in 2005 Canadians were once again committed to the struggle in Afghanistan. By the summer of 2006 Canadian combat forces had deployed south to the volatile and extremely dangerous Kandahar Province and became actively involved in the fight for that country. But after all, as the outspoken CDS, General Hillier, observed, "Canadians have never flinched in the face of danger."[33]

Subsequently, as part of Operation Archer, it fell to the 1st Battalion, the PPCLI or Task Force (TF) Orion, as its CO, Lieutenant-Colonel Ian Hope, titled it, to conduct the combat tasks in Kandahar Province.[34] Their mission read, benignly enough, "Task Force Orion will assist Afghans in the establishment of good governance, security and stability, and reconstruction in the province of Kandahar during Op Archer Rotation (Roto) 1 in order to help extend the legitimacy and credibility of the Government of Afghanistan throughout the Islamic Republic of Afghanistan and at the same time help to establish conditions necessary for NATO Stage 3 expansion."[35] The execution of the mission, however, would be far from benign.

CHAPTER TWO:

A Growing Storm

THE BRUNT OF THE fight to pacify the southern region of Afghanistan fell to Lieutenant-Colonel Hope's TF Orion. Few realized exactly how desperate that fight would actually be. On arrival to Kandahar, the CO intended for his BG to become an extension of the efforts being exerted by the Canadian PRT in Kandahar City. Hope had a vast area to cover, approximately 54,000 square kilometres. He broke his BG into company groups, which were the core elements of his TF. Hope explained, "We needed to make up for lack of numbers by being constantly aggressive and dynamic."[1] Each was as self-contained as possible and consisted of approximately 150 riflemen augmented by engineers, military police, a forward observation officer (FOO) party, and civilian military affairs (CIMIC) officers.

Each company group had to be able to operate independently for long periods of time. The CO also stressed flexibility and explained to his company commanders that it was necessary that they be able to adapt to the situation on the ground. "Don't be template about doctrine," insisted Hope. "Do what works."[2] And with that advice, he pushed his sub-units out into autonomous forward operating bases (FOBs) located in areas that would allow them to work with Afghan National Security Forces (ANSF) and district leaders to improve governance, security, and socio-economic conditions in key districts of the province. Hope instructed his task force elements to engage village, district, and provincial leaders in order to convince them to implement GoA initiatives. The BG committed itself to this "3D" (Development, Diplomacy, and Defence) whole of government approach.

An added challenge facing TF Orion, which had moved to southern Afghanistan under the U.S. led OEF mission, was that it would also have to make the difficult transition from an American command and control framework to an ISAF command model partway through their rotation when the Americans transferred responsibility for the area to NATO as part of the alliance's Phase 3 expansion.[3] As part of that transition, Brigadier-General David Fraser would take command of the southern region — including the province of Kandahar for which the PPCLI BG was responsible. Fraser would also have under his jurisdiction the other southern provinces, including the hot spots of Helmand and Uruzgan provinces, an area measuring 220,744 square kilometres. In essence, the Canadians would be the bridge between the current U.S. led OEF mission and NATO's ISAF mission.[4]

Nonetheless, for TF Orion the tour began quietly, almost too quietly, with many of the troops complaining that they had not yet "closed with the enemy." The young soldiers craved action — they wanted to see combat and the endless framework patrolling and leader engagements became rather mundane to many. However, as the adage goes, "be careful of what you wish for." As winter turned to spring, the traditional Afghan fighting campaign season began and TF Orion initiated what would be a long series of events leading to a very cataclysmic encounter between Canadian and Taliban forces in the killing fields of Panjwayi.

The surge in activity occurred June 2006. It quickly became evident that the steady increase in Taliban activity was indicative of a full-blown offensive. Consequently, the 1 PPCLI BG began focusing its energies on security operations, specifically to find, fix, and destroy the enemy. Hope deployed his manoeuvre forces in a dispersed, dynamic, and flexible manner. The troops lived amongst the Afghans to gain their trust and to keep the Taliban off-balance. The TF leaders utilized coalition intelligence and sensors to try and pinpoint the enemy. They also used human intelligence (HUMINT) gathered from local nationals.[5] All of this information, distilled with intuition, shaped the decisions Hope and his subordinate commanders made in regard to finding the enemy. Once the enemy was located, they attempted "to manoeuvre into that district quietly under the cover of darkness, using deception, and — as much as possible — isolate the village by using thin blocking and cut off forces." The CO explained, "We would conduct manoeuvre (cordon and searches) and fires (show of force with artillery or 25mm fire) to produce enemy ICOM [Intercepted communications] chatter, and from this ICOM chatter (or HUMINT from local nationals), we would attempt to vector in upon the enemy locations." But in the end, Hope conceded, "finding him [the enemy] was almost always a result of advance-to-contact in the close country where he hid and was confirmed by the exchange of fire at close quarters."[6] He added:

> We trained ourselves to hold and fix the enemy with whatever we could bring in, as close as 100 metres. We resisted the tendency to withdraw back to our last safe place. But, finishing the enemy was difficult. They [Taliban] were very good at slipping away. You could drop as much ordnance as you wanted but in the end to finish the enemy you had to walk the ground — it was always a close quarter fight.[7]

Not surprisingly, TF Orion conducted a large number of operations in Kandahar Province. "We were the 'fire battalion' for the brigade," quipped Captain Kevin Barry. "We would be sent out to put down a contact somewhere and would do it and then another fire would start up somewhere else and we would be sent there."[8] But ominously, the "troops-in-contact" (TICs) in the Pashmul area took on a ferocity that was foreboding.

Operation Mountain Thrust, mounted between 15 May and 31 July 2006, initiated the looming showdown. It was a major coalition offensive that spanned the five southern and several eastern provinces. "Operation Mountain Thrust," explained Lieutenant-Colonel Shane Schreiber, the operations officer for the Multinational Brigade Headquarters (MNB HQ), "the precursor to NATO's Regional Command (South) (RC [S]) HQ, was [intended] to defeat the Taliban in their traditional areas." The scope of the mission, he lamented, "was like digging a hole in the ocean — it was difficult to secure an area. Once an area was secure we hoped that the ANA would [continue to] secure it — but once we left the Taliban filled back in."[9] Not only did the Taliban slip back in, but they did so in increasing numbers.

Nonetheless, the operation demonstrated 1 PPCLI BG's manoeuvrability and aggressive spirit. On numerous occasions the BG spun on its axis and responded to urgent calls for assistance. The task force certainly impressed their superiors. "To be able to turn a BG around in less than 12 hours and cover 160 kilometres through hostile territory in order to link up with the Afghan National Police and reinforce those district centres," asserted the brigade commander, "that is no small feat and it showed great agility on the part of Task Force Orion."[10] The CO, Lieutenant-Colonel Hope boasted, "We demonstrated the capability of an all-arms force." He added, "We have taken every task given to us, and proven that we can operate anywhere in southern Afghanistan, with anyone."[11]

But the ability of the TF to conduct its operations with the speed and flexibility they demonstrated was due to their light armoured vehicle (LAV) III, 17 ton, eight-wheeled armoured personnel carriers, which were built in London, Ontario, by General Dynamics Land Systems. The approximately seven metres long and 2.81 metres high monsters entered CF service in 1999. The vehicles require a crew of three and carry seven soldiers with all their equipment. The powerful LAV has a top end speed of 100 kilometres per hour and a range of 500 kilometres. It was also heavily armed. The LAV boasts a 25 mm Bushmaster chain gun, a 7.62 mm general-purpose machine gun (GPMG), a 5.56 mm pintle-mounted machine gun, and eight smoke grenade launchers. The robust vehicle, called the "Dragon that shits white men" by the Taliban, also proved capable of repelling amazing amounts of enemy fire. Its sloped hull was designed to deflect the blast of mines and IEDs, saving numerous lives. In all, the vehicles have been proven capable of withstanding the punishing terrain, dust, and constant use of Afghan combat, and were held in the highest esteem and trust by the Canadian soldiers who use them.

Despite the TF's aggressive posture and fighting spirit, the situation did not improve. Between May and June there was an alarming increase in the number of TICs. In addition, the Taliban began to confiscate cellphones from local nationals as a counter-intelligence measure. They also established plans for setting up checkpoints and moving into Kandahar City. On 30 June 2006, the task force received reports indicating that the Taliban were issuing night letters directing Afghan locals to leave the Panjwayi and Zhari areas immediately as Taliban elements were planning to engage GoA forces and CF elements.

The state of chaos and violence reached such levels that by June 2006 the Senlis Council reported, "In Kandahar, Canadian troops are fighting increasingly deadly counter-insurgency operations under Operation Enduring Freedom against the resurgent Taliban ... Kandahar now is a war zone, with suicide bombings, rocket attacks, ambushes and repeated outbreaks of open warfare, resulting in numerous Canadian fatalities and many more injuries."[12] They concluded, "Kandahar is a province at war: there is no peace to keep."[13] Statistics backed their assertions. By June 2006, there was a "600 % increase in violent attacks in the last six months, and terrorism is now a pressing concern in Kandahar; the majority of terror attacks in Afghanistan occur in Kandahar and bordering provinces."[14]

In July, due to the increasing Taliban presence and activity, Lieutenant-Colonel Hope developed a concept of operations in Pashmul to "disrupt the Taliban in Zhari District through concentration of combat power and isolation and clearance of objective Puma in the vicinity of the village of Pashmul." He explained, "The clearance of Puma will be conducted by deliberate cordon and searches of areas assessed to contain Taliban and/or their caches based on previous intelligence and current HUMINT gained by Afghan National Security Forces (ANSF) partnered with TF Orion for this operation."[15]

The Taliban, however, refused to go quietly. "Well we know we're heading into the shit now," exclaimed Sergeant Mike Denine when he witnessed the procession of civilians fleeing the town with their meagre possessions.[16]

Captain Andrew Charchuk, the FOO for "C" Coy Group, 1 PPCLI, drew the same conclusion. "As we arrived closer to the objective area we saw the women and children pouring out of the town," described Charchuk. "Not a good sign," he added, describing that they "pushed on and about 3 kilometres from our intended line of departure to start the operation [at around 0030 hours] we were ambushed by Taliban fighters ... I saw about 20 RPGs [rocket-propelled grenades] all bursting in the air over the LAVs. It was an unreal scene to describe. There was no doubt we were in a big fight."[17]

That contact initiated a larger sequence of events. The TF fought hard in the 50° Celsius heat in a running battle that lasted for days. As embedded reporter Christie Blatchford summarized, "July was a daily diet of long battles that went on for hours and stretched the battle group thin over six hundred kilometres in seven separate districts over some of the most treacherous terrain in Afghanistan."[18]

By August, intelligence reports continued to paint a picture of ongoing Taliban activity, namely key leader engagements and increasing TICs, all of which indicated that the enemy was massing forces in the Panjwayi Valley. The Taliban focus on the area was not hard to understand. Panjwayi has always been critically important to the Taliban because it is a fertile, densely populated, and economically lucrative area. It has also been the traditional staging area for attacks against Kandahar City, as well as a resupply area for troops staging in Zhari District.

In addition, Kandahar Province and its capital, Kandahar City, have always been of interest to the Taliban because the region has consistently maintained a kind of autonomy from any of the various central governments in Kabul. It is also the second largest province in Afghanistan, located in the harsh, barren, desert environment of the volatile southeastern corner of the country. It is bounded on the north and northeast by the mountainous Uruzgan and Zabul Provinces and in the west by Helmand Province, and it shares a very porous 402 kilometre-long border with the Pakistan province of Baluchistan. Kandahar City is situated at the junction of Afghanistan's main highways and is the major southern link to Pakistan. In fact, the highway system passes from Spin Boldak on the Pakistan border, through Kandahar City to Kabul. Moreover, Kandahar was the birthplace and continues to be the heartland of the Taliban itself.

Kandahar had become the centre of gravity for the Government of Afghanistan and the coalition, as well as the Taliban, in the fight for the confidence and support of Afghans. As Lieutenant-Colonel Schreiber explained, "[We] began to develop Afghan development zones (ADZ) to create a secure bubble around a nucleus where we could push resources and redevelopment (i.e., ink spot method)"[19] These efforts were all part of the governance, security, and reconstruction strategy for rebuilding a modern Afghanistan. For the Taliban, victory in Kandahar Province would discredit the GoA and coalition forces in the eyes of Afghans. Consequently, "We were convinced that the Taliban were massing in Panjwayi to establish a permanent base of operations there, with a view to attacking Kandahar City," confirmed Lieutenant-Colonel Ian Hope.[20]

And the Taliban was intent on winning. "The Taliban emptied Quetta and other centres to conduct offensive operations in Regional Command (RC) South in 2006," confided Schreiber. "It was a window of opportunity for them as we focused on elections and the hand-over from U.S. control in Kandahar to NATO control as part of Stage 3 expansion."[21] The American and NATO focus on these activities provided the Taliban with an ideal opportunity to achieve success. "Our intelligence," revealed Schreiber, "estimated that they [Taliban] brought in, as a minimum, 12,000 foot soldiers."[22]

In early August continuing reports of major enemy activity and massing of troops triggered yet another coalition foray into the area. On 3 August 2006, Lieutenant-Colonel Hope and his BG found themselves in the Pashmul/Panjwayi area once again.

The day started ominously. In the inky darkness of pre-dawn the lead assault platoon snaked its way silently through a wadi, using thermal sights. The objective was a bazaar comprised of eight to 12 buildings. Suddenly the assault platoon opened a concentrated fire shattering the early morning calm. They had identified Taliban fighters in early warning positions a scant 150 metres from their vehicles. As they rolled forward in their LAV IIIs, the lead vehicle struck a pressure-plate-activated improvised explosive device (IED) killing two of the soldiers inside. Evidence indicated additional IEDs, half-buried in the soft ground, covered the restricted axis of advance, leading to a narrow bridge that was surrounded by fighting positions.

"The enemy had emplaced five IEDs along a 100-metre stretch of road coming out of the wadi and up to a short bridge crossing a small canal," described Lieutenant-Colonel Hope. "This was heavily canalized terrain. The thick mud walls on the sides of the narrow roads had been loop-holed so that the enemy could fire upon us from multiple directions without exposing themselves."[23] In addition, numerous irrigation ditches (four to six feet deep, most covered with grass) provided even more cover for the enemy.

The task force plan was amended and a dismounted approach in conjunction with the ANSF was undertaken. Quickly, TF Orion soldiers advanced and seized a schoolhouse. In the process they had unknowingly sprung a Taliban trap. The Canadian soldiers soon found themselves hammered from three sides as the Taliban quickly tried to seize the opportunity to kill and capture them. "You know, I wouldn't say it was farmers dropping their shovels by the way they operated," reminisced Master-Corporal Matthew Parsons. "They knew tactics, they knew how to get on our flanks, they knew how to use fire and manoeuvre." Parsons concluded, "They were smart, they were a smart crew."[24] Another soldier noted, "These guys [enemy] know what they're doing. They know how to ambush, they know fire and movement. They know everything we do."[25] It had become apparent to these Canadian veterans of southern Afghanistan that the Taliban they were now fighting were different, more tenacious and experienced, than those they had fought on and off all summer in Panjwayi.

Hope recalled, "We trained ourselves to hold and fix the enemy with whatever we could bring in, including artillery as close as 100 metres ... we resisted the tendency to withdraw back to last safe place." The commanding officer shrugged, "You could drop as much ordnance as you wanted [but] in the end to finish the enemy you had to walk the ground — it was always a close quarter fight ... Finishing the enemy was difficult. They [Taliban] were very good at slipping away."[26]

But that day the Taliban had no intention of leaving. The fight became desperate. One soldier described it "as a well-planned ambush." He recounted how stealthy Taliban forces formed a horseshoe around Canadian troops holed up in the tiny schoolhouse, surrounded by land mines, then launched a volley of rocket-propelled grenades. As the soldier poked his head out of a doorway a grenade swished by him and scorched his forearm. He turned to watch the grenade strike a wall; the ensuing spray of shrapnel killed three of his comrades. "They were too organized," asserted the soldier, "we had to pull back."[27]

Another participant, Sergeant Patrick Towers, later acknowledged that the Taliban were determined to win and fought bravely.

> I underestimated them because I figured them to be just a bunch of farmers that pick up AK-47s but they employ tactics, they have training and what blew me away was later, when we swept their ambush positions, they had depth to their positions, cut-offs with machine guns, anti-tank positions — all dug-in, as well as a casualty collection point ... They were well trained and they can employ tactics ... They're certainly not just a bunch of dirt farmers.[28]

Sergeant Towers was not the only one to have underestimated the enemy. The Taliban, conceded Brigadier-General David Fraser, the ISAF MNB Commander, "was more sophisticated at what he was doing than we had originally thought."[29]

Ominously, the SOF linguist attached to the BG to monitor radio intercepts for the operation confirmed "the Taliban were confident they could hold the ground." Based on the amount of enemy radio chatter, he assessed "there had to be 900 to 1,200 insurgents in the area." [30]

As the situation transformed from desperate to precarious even the seriously wounded manned their weapons to hold back the advancing Taliban. Hope received a desperate call for assistance from one of his subordinate officers. The message was simple and direct — the officer informed his CO that "if they did not get LAVs up there now, they would all die."[31]

Lieutenant-Colonel Hope pushed fresh troops forward. All braved the fire to assist their comrades. At the same time, in nearby Kandahar City, a suicide bomber attacked Hope's recovery convoy, on its way to provide assistance and pull the damaged LAVs off the battlefield. Hope realized "that we were enveloped, and that the enemy were coordinating their efforts to trap and annihilate us."[32] The CO once again realized how "everything in Afghanistan submits to incredible friction."[33]

The situation was tenuous at best and the commanding officer needed to regain the initiative so that he could withdraw his forces. Hope later recounted, "It is as if in the middle of a lonely fight for life, the hand of a true angel descended to give us decisive help."[34] During the frenetic struggle to hold the Taliban at bay an American B-1 Bomber that had already dropped their ordnance elsewhere, but heard Hope's desperate calls for assistance, passed dangerously low at less than 500 feet over the insurgents' positions and lit their afterburners, creating an explosion that reverberated through the battlefield, providing an enormous boost to the Canadians and cowing the Taliban. That air support, and the assistance of French Mirage fighter jets, turned the tide and returned the initiative to the Canadians. However, with light fading and the absence of any ANSF troops to hold the ground once taken, Hope decided to pull back. He also realized that the Taliban had returned in strength and it had now become a larger operation, beyond his unit, to dislodge them.[35] The concept of Operation Medusa was born in the heat, death, and destruction of the 3 August battle.

"The cost [of the 3 August battle] was significant," conceded Fraser. But he insisted, "We picked it ... we, being the Afghan government, picked the fight. They had information that there was Taliban there so we picked the conditions and went in after them."[36] The brigade commander explained how they had been in Panjwayi a couple of times before with TF Orion and "we knew it was an important area for the Taliban ... However, we didn't have enough forces to go in there earlier for a sustained offensive effort, other than what we conducted with Lieutenant-Colonel Hope's battle group."[37]

He acknowledged what most had come to suspect. He indicated the "scale of Taliban activity made it clear we would have to come back." In fact, he described:

> It was 3 August when we went in there and lost a couple of guys. We received intelligence of major activity, that's why Hope was going back in there. We knew it was big and Lieutenant-Colonel Hope went in and got hit hard in the objective area. We met after that and analysed what happened. The Taliban used two improvised

34

explosive device (IED) attacks roughly in the centre of the objective area, as well as RPGs. Our assessment was that the Taliban had gone into the Pashmul area, specifically the Bazar-e-Panjwayi area, dug in, and now he was prepared to fight. Quite frankly, the Taliban was everything we thought and more. In fact, he was more sophisticated at what he was doing than we originally thought. So we analysed all that, figured out where he was and what he was doing and came to the assessment that he was acting as a conventional force. We then asked ourselves one question: what was the enemy's intent?[38]

Brigadier-General Fraser pondered the problem. Fraser believed Panjwayi was going to be the Taliban's "major fight for the summer." He explained, "the third of August was the defining day that we knew exactly what we were facing, and what the enemy wanted to do, the enemy's intent."[39] In Fraser's estimation, the enemy's intent "was to isolate Kandahar City, not directly but indirectly, to demonstrate the weakness and the inability of the national Government to come after them with a conventional force."[40] He stated, "This also indicated to us that the Taliban were actually progressing with the evolution of their own operations to the next stage[41] where they thought they were capable enough to go and challenge the national government and coalition forces in a conventional manner."[42]

Fraser added, "We also assessed that their intent was to engage the international community in a battle of attrition on ground of their tactical choosing to cause as many casualties as they could to attack our centre of gravity (i.e., domestic public support)."[43] He concluded that the Taliban plan "was designed to defeat us from a 'political will' point of view; to illustrate weakness in the Government of Afghanistan and thereby set the stage where the Taliban could attack the city and defeat not only the provincial government there but also attack the national government in Afghanistan in a fairly sophisticated and substantive way."[44] As a result, Fraser briefed his plan to Lieutenant-General David Richards, the British commander then in charge of NATO's forces in Afghanistan at NATO headquarters. "I said this is a fight we can't lose," remembered Fraser. "This is the main, main fight."[45]

CHAPTER THREE:

Genesis of an Operation

With the Canadian BG bloodied and bruised from its latest incursion into Pashmul, it became clear to commanders and staffs that the problem was now larger than most had anticipated. It was a brigade operation. As Brigadier-General Fraser had counselled his superiors, it was now "the main, main fight."[1] The enemy had proven to be tenacious and skilled; they had decided to dig-in and fight. Ominously, they were massing for a potential strike at Kandahar City itself, which would prove politically crippling, if not fatal, to the Government of Afghanistan and the coalition. Fraser and his staff knew they had to develop an effective plan.

ISAF headquarters assigned the Multinational Brigade (MNB) the mission of defeating the Taliban in Pashmul in order to set the conditions for the establishment of the Kandahar Afghan Development Zone (ADZ).[2] Fraser realized as a commander he had to answer three critical questions: What is it I am facing? What if something happens? What must I do next? He felt that answering those three basic questions would assist with his phasing of the operation. It also helped him "deal with an asymmetric enemy."[3] Subsequently, Fraser issued his intent, which was: to disrupt the Taliban in the district; achieve security for the local population and freedom of manoeuvre for aid agencies; complete Quick Impact Projects (QIPs) to achieve rapid reconstruction; and subsequently develop the region's governance and economic capacity. He developed a scheme of manoeuvre that involved four phases:

1. shape the battlefield to disrupt Taliban forces through the conduct of leadership engagements, brigade manoeuvres, and the intensive application of air and indirect fires (e.g., fighter aircraft, Spectre C-130 gunships, artillery);

2. conduct operations (i.e., decisive strike, link-up, and secure the area of operations [AO]) to clear enemy out of Pashmul/Panjwayi;

3. exploit success to the west of Panjwayi to create a secure zone for the ADZ; and

4. conduct stabilization operations and reconstruction to support the return and security of the population in the region.[4]

Retrospectively, Fraser acknowledged that "in Phase 1, we spent a lot of time planning and gathering intelligence."[5] Lieutenant-Colonel Peter Williams, the joint effects coordination officer, recalled, "The threat was generally a very conventional one so we devoted a lot of time toward developing target packs."[6] In essence, the idea was to get "a very clear picture of what was in there," according to Captain Chris Purdy, the TF 3-06 intelligence officer. He explained:

> We then wanted to conduct a feint in order to get the Taliban to light up their C2 nodes, to get the Taliban to reinforce so we could see them moving into their forward positions. And then when they did that we would strike them. And the feint, the way we conceived to do the feint, to get the same reaction that we did on the last two times we went in there [i.e., TF Orion] was to use the same scheme of manoeuvre, essentially a company from the north, and a company from the south, the same methodology that Ian Hope had used and we hoped to get the same reaction. We had a lot of fire power. So we thought we were going to be successful in doing that. [The theory was] once we had done that and we'd essentially reduced the Taliban defense in there[i.e., Pashmul/Panjwayi] to small isolated pockets, we would

then conduct a link- up of the companies moving north to south and south to north respectively and clear the remaining pockets out.[7]

The plan lacked one major component — combat forces. The MNB operations officer, Lieutenant-Colonel Shane Schreiber, acknowledged, "We were spread pretty thin on the ground between Martello, Spin Boldak, Kandahar City and Panjwayi. Therefore, we wanted to do was concentrate that BG and essentially fix the Taliban in Pashmul to make sure that they couldn't push any further into Kandahar or Highway 1." He described how that they had hoped to use the coalition's superior ISR (intelligence, surveillance, reconnaissance) assets and firepower to "begin to pull apart the nodes and take apart the Taliban defense." But Schreiber conceded, "We didn't have enough [combat power] to clear it … At that point we assessed it would have taken a brigade attack and there was no way we were ever going to generate a four, or even a three BG brigade to be able to do that." Schreiber quickly added, "Nor did we want to because of the collateral damage that would have caused. So instead, what we decided to do was to defeat the Taliban build-up by isolating and disrupting and pulling the Taliban apart in chunks, hoping that at some point they would say 'okay it's not worth it.'"[8]

Schreiber was referring to the hired guns, the day fighters — those who fought for the Taliban for money and were not necessarily committed to the cause. The coalition hoped that those fighters would drift away leaving only the "level one" or hard-core Taliban, who would then concentrate in smaller numbers, allowing the coalition to destroy them.[9] Brigadier-General Fraser believed this was the core of the plan. "Initially, we thought there was 500 enemy in the 'pocket' — 200 hard core, 300 tier two [i.e., local hired guns versus ideological fanatics] and my intent for Phase 2 was to engage the Taliban forces over a prolonged period of time with lethal fires (e.g., fast air, artillery) … That would entice the less dedicated, you know, the tier two types, to give up the fight." Fraser stressed, "I wanted to impact those individuals who had joined up to go in for a couple of days, you know, get paid a few bucks, have a few wins [i.e., successful attacks/inflict casualties on coalition forces] and then leave. I was going to draw out the fight with long-range fires as long as I could and go after their minds, realizing that it would then be harder for their commanders to keep them [tier 2 fighters] motivated and keep them going ... So this was all about time, patience, perseverance, and not rushing into it. We had no intention of rushing into it."[10]

In essence, Fraser's intent was to separate the Taliban forces by putting deliberate kinetic and non-kinetic pressure on them. "We had them contained. They were fixing themselves, or rather they had fixed themselves." Fraser explained, "They were bringing forces in from everywhere — infiltrating through the Reg[estan] Desert, up from Pakistan and they assembled a lot of commanders in the pocket." However, he emphasized, "We were controlling the agenda. The only thing that the Taliban had to decide was if they wanted to speed up the agenda, which they tried to do at the end."[11]

No one was fooled by the effort it would take to clear the Taliban from the region. The challenge was imposing. Schreiber conceded

> Essentially, especially after the 3 August attack [by Lieutenant-Colonel Hope's BG], we realized that we were facing a battalion size defensive position based upon complex obstacles covered by surveillance, indirect and direct fire and incorporating kill zones ... So this is what we faced: two company positions with strong points from which they [Taliban] would sally forth to conduct ambushes along Highway 1. We were having anywhere between three to five ambushes a day on Highway 1, every day late July and early August ... and then they had another company defensive position to control the Arghandab River with a C2 [command and control] node in the middle.[12]

The result was the brigade and BG staffs devoting a great deal of effort to Phase 1 planning and gathering intelligence. Subsequently, the emphasis shifted in the early stages of Phase 2 to "building up" — specifically to assembling the combat forces and enablers (e.g., ISR platforms, aviation, close air support (CAS), direct and indirect fire assets), as well as the necessary logistical support.

The Taliban had chosen to build-up and posture themselves in a way that directly challenged the GoA and NATO forces in a conventional manner, namely by digging-in, building fortifications, and holding ground. Despite this brazen but arguably foolish decision (due to the coalition's firepower), the Taliban were not about to make it easy to target them. The enemy operated in teams of roughly platoon equivalent size (i.e., 20–30 fighters) over which effective command and control was maintained. As they had already shown, and would further confirm, they were sophisticated enough to conduct tactical reliefs-in-place and coordinated attacks against their opponents. More importantly, their defences were prepared as strong points, which made extensive use of natural and man-made obstacles and all had interlocking arcs of direct fire with small arms, RPGs, and recoilless rifles. Their indirect mortar fire was responsive and well coordinated. Obstacles on roads were particularly prevalent, with extensive use of pressure-plate IEDs. For example, in a 50-metre span of road leading into a Taliban defensive position five such devices were found. They also widened the existing canal with light equipment so that it could act as a tank trap.

It was the Taliban's excellent use of fieldcraft that removed some of the vulnerability they imposed on themselves by engaging in a conventional attritional battle. Trench lines were prepared by hand and superbly concealed to evade detection by ground and airborne ISR assets. Trenches were tied into thick mud walls that proved extremely resilient against both direct fire weapons (i.e., 25mm cannon and small arms) and C4 explosives. In fact, they had developed a sophisticated strongpoint replete with entrenchments that resembled a Soviet defensive position. Communications trenches were dug to connect the larger trench system and bunkers. Lieutenant-Colonel Schreiber concluded, "[the Taliban] had a battalion defensive position fully dug-in with complex robust command and control capability with mutually supporting positions and advanced surveillance and early warning."[13]

The Taliban was highly motivated and fought in place. Their fire discipline was strictly imposed in order to draw coalition forces into their kill zones and they aggressively launched counterattacks from the flanks with small mobile teams to attack the depth of assaulting forces. Finally, an army report also noted that their gunnery, "particularly with the SPG [73mm / 82mm recoilless rifle] was very good resulting in the defeat of a LAV 3 and support vehicles during one assault."[14]

Undeniably, the Taliban had chosen their ground well. Beyond the fortifications they had built, the natural lay of the land worked in their favour. Pashmul is a greenbelt with thick vegetation. Seven-foot-high marijuana fields hid movement and masked the thermal imagery of the LAV.[15] As one official report noted:

> The terrain was extremely difficult due to the combination of natural and built up features. Enemy defences were anchored on the Arghandab River that provided a natural impediment to high-speed manoeuvre to the defensive position. Although dried up for the most part, the steepness of the banks canalized movement to fording sites where we were vulnerable to enemy direct and indirect fires. Canals criss-crossed the manoeuvre space and proved an impediment to off-road movement for LAVs. Corn and marijuana fields (with stalks extending to a height of 6–8 feet) limited visibility and provided excellent concealment for both TB [Taliban] fighters and natural obstacles. The most significant terrain features were arguably the mud walls and the vineyards. Mud walls approximately eight feet high and two feet thick dominated the terrain. In one case 10 blocks of C4 were required for a single breach. The vineyards covered earth mounds approximately 3–5 feet high with rows arranged every three feet.[16]

Captain Chris Purdy echoed the assessment of the enemy's careful choice of ground. "The enemy actually had a fairly high level of command

and control," he emphasized, "and it became obvious to see how they would manoeuvre around the area." He believed the Taliban objective would be "to suck us right into the heart of Pashmul where we could be engaged dismounted … The enemy was very afraid of the LAVs. They called them tanks, the green monsters, a number of terms, but they were quite aware that the LAV is a hard thing to engage." Purdy appraised, "They had two aims: one was to suck us into a dismounted battle where they could effectively kill a large number of our soldiers, and also to suck the LAVs into an area where they can be engaged with mortars and the 82 mm recoilless rifles."[17]

Clearly, the imposing challenges of both the natural terrain and the tenacity and preparation of the enemy required careful preparation. Brigadier-General Fraser explained, "A lot of effort was devoted in Phase 2 to building up, assembling the enablers and forces we required, as well as the logistical support … In addition, we attempted to lure the Taliban out so we could determine their exact size, location and engage them." His intent was not to launch Phase 2, the actual ground attack, until "we decided we were ready and the Taliban were severely weakened."[18] Having determined the Taliban's intent, Fraser was determined to control the conduct and tempo of the battle. He explained:

> So I made an assessment and I thought, "Okay, they've gone conventional, this is their intent, so how do we defeat their intent." Well, I decided that we will defeat their intent by putting our forces all around them and we will wait them out. You see, they wanted us to get into a battle of attrition, to slug it out, to try and clear them out of that complex terrain where they have all the advantageous of a well dug-in and protected force — where our technological superiority could be nullified. I directed that we would wait them out. I reversed the roles on them. The Taliban went conventional and ISAF went unconventional. I decided that we would manoeuvre, feint and slap a cordon around them. We would engage them in a battle of attrition, but it would be on our terms, namely a battle of attrition through joint fires.

We anticipated that the enemy had two courses of action. One was that they would just continue to move around and we would continue to attack them. The second enemy course of action, the most dangerous, was if they attacked. This is what they did — they continually challenged us on the fringes of the terrain that held and fortified. Nonetheless, I wanted to wait for two to three weeks, all the while hammering them with fires and then eventually when I thought the time was right, when the enemy was physically and psychologically weak, then go in and seize the objective areas we had identified in the Pashmul area.[19]

Fraser deployed his forces around the objective area to provide as much containment as he could. The containment force maintained a dynamic disposition in order to provoke the enemy to move inside the "circle so we could shape the battle and advantageously engage the enemy."[20] Coalition forces also dropped psychological pamphlets to warn and encourage non-combatants/civilians and less fanatical enemy personnel to vacate the area. "For the three weeks before we launched Operation Medusa, we talked to and gave money to every village leader in the area," revealed Fraser. "In exchange, we asked them to get rid of the Taliban." He conceded, "We had limited success."[21]

Brigadier-General Fraser briefed General Richards on the plan for Operation Medusa. In turn, the ISAF Commander confirmed to Fraser that Operation Medusa was the ISAF main effort. In fact, he went even further and pronounced that Operation Medusa was actually the "NATO main effort."[22] That sentiment was supported by NATO Secretary General Jaap de Hoop Scheffer, who publically announced, "If we fail and this nation becomes a failed state again, the consequences will be felt in Ottawa, in Brussels, in the Hague, in Madrid, in New York and elsewhere. That is what is at stake."[23]

Scheffer's pronouncement of risk and his perceived importance of the operation were of little help. Coalition forces were spread very thinly around the cordon. Despite the rhetoric being espoused at the highest levels of NATO regarding the importance of the looming battle, the action would be a largely Canadian fight. "Promises of *in extremis* assistance were a placebo to take the sting away from the constant 'no' that always came following requests to send troops to the south, and meant nothing," stated General Hillier. "We were," he angrily recalled, "essentially in it by ourselves."[24] The Americans and British were already engaged in combat elsewhere in Afghanistan and were hard-pressed to assist, although they did what they could. The Europeans failed their allies and refused to participate. The Dutch declined to assist in the actual combat but did take over FOB Martello, which freed up additional Canadian resources that were fed into the battle.[25]

But the problems did not stop with the shortage of combat troops. Brigadier-General Fraser lamented, "There are a lot of challenges working within any coalition [e.g., national agendas, different SOPs, TTPs, languages, staff procedures], however, the biggest challenge in Afghanistan is that you very quickly learn that NATO in itself has virtually none, or very little, of the necessary combat enablers." He continued:

> For instance, I briefed the commander of ISAF personally on the context of my operations for Operation Medusa. He [Richards] in turn confirmed to me that I was ISAF's, no actually he said NATO's, main effort. As a result, one would think okay, it seems like the commander supports everything so I should be given the support I need. However, that isn't necessarily the case because NATO doesn't own the enablers. The enablers for the most part are still owned by their contributing countries and here in Afghanistan, largely the enablers that we're looking at are aviation, air and ISR and they are still American or British, and to some degree in this theatre Dutch. So, even though he says you are the main effort, you still have to convince those countries that you are the main effort. And if they are reluctant, NATO doesn't even necessarily have the hammer to direct, for sake of example, the British to provide this and the

Americans to provide that. So that was the first real big thing I noticed. As a result, there was a lot of begging. I know that the Multi National Brigade and even the Commander of ISAF had to go and do a lot of groveling to and bartering to get the required assets shifted over to our operation. And the effect it had on me though was that the enablers that did become available had restrictions on them. For instance I was told, okay you can have these things for x-amount of days, but then they're being shifted back to whatever region again.[26]

In the end, Brigadier-General Fraser bemoaned, "The national caveats in NATO are killing me, they are really killing me." He noted, "We found out what NATO could not do. We simply couldn't get everyone we needed … The Germans wouldn't come down here; the French company weren't allowed to come down here; and I couldn't get the Italians …We did get the Portuguese to come into the Kandahar Airfield to help out with static security tasks but most NATO countries came out with national caveats that precluded them from assisting us in actually fighting in Pashmul."

As one senior Canadian officer later described of Operation Medusa, "We were basically told you're on your fucking own for a while."[27]

The lack of allied participation was not only frustrating, it was also shocking considering what was at stake. As Fraser elaborated:

The idea of failing here [i.e., not defeating the Taliban in Pashmul] was unacceptable. You want to talk about pressure, this was about a city [Kandahar City], a country, an alliance, and Canada was right in the middle of it, both from a battle group and from a brigade point of view. The battle was everything and failure was not an option. This was not just an attack; it was not just an operational fight; it was a NATO fight, it was everything and the more that we got into this fight, the more the pink cards — the un-stated national caveats started to

46

creep into it. The more we got into the fight, the more we found that this was exactly what NATO was built for. This was almost Cold War-like type of fighting. It was conventional fighting.[28]

Fraser was not alone in his assessment. The CDS explained, "All of the sudden in 2006, we found ourselves in the middle of a war ... we found ourselves up against a determined and tough enemy." General Hillier noted that "the Taliban were massing against Canadian and other NATO forces, trying to take over Kandahar City and discredit NATO, discredit Canada and probably cause the fall of the Afghan government itself."[29]

But not everyone was prepared to participate. As Fraser began to line up his formation to do battle he realized he was starkly alone. He had a plan, but not the forces necessary to execute it. He would need to adapt and quickly because the main fight was approaching faster than he or anyone else wished. And no one had any false expectations. As Lieutenant-Colonel Schreiber bluntly acknowledged, "We knew we had a real hard nut to crack."[30]

LAV IIIs operating in the lush Pashmul district. The 17-ton, eight-wheeled armoured vehicle proved to be a robust, reliable workhorse that won the affection and trust of the troops.

Despite the LAV III's 2.81-metre height, for those in the turret observation was often obscured by the tall corn and marijuana fields.

Courtesy 1 RCR BG.

Typical farmland in Pashmul showing the lush foliage, mud walls, and formidable and dominating grape-drying huts.

Courtesy Combat Camera, negative AR20006-P005-0025.

Canadian soldiers moving through dense foliage.

A company leaguer. The "G-Wagon" is the small jeep-like vehicle to the right of the photograph.

ANA soldiers.

Afghan National Police patrol stopped by Canadian soldiers and ANA. The ANP were extremely unprofessional and unreliable. They often wore no formal uniform and were difficult to identify as ANSF.

The twin peaks at Ma'Sūm Ghar that were focal points of the 19 August battle.

Psychological Operations pamphlet used to influence insurgents. The text in Pashto reads "fight and die, surrender and live."

Psychological Operations pamphlet explaining to insurgents how to correctly surrender to avoid possible injury.

Top: The town of Bazar-e-Panjwayi.

Lieutenant-Colonel Omer Lavoie, CO TF 3-06.

Aerial view of the Arghandab River watershed and surrounding Pashmul countryside.

Aerial view of the "saw-toothed" white schoolhouse in Bayenzi.

The infamous white schoolhouse.

Pounding Objective Rugby.

CHAPTER FOUR:

Opening Salvos

THE FIGHT FOR PASHMUL, or more accurately for Afghanistan, as Brigadier-General Fraser and other senior NATO military leaders described, no longer rested with Hope and TF Orion. Their tour was quickly coming to an end and by early August they were already conducting a relief in place (RIP) with the 1st Battalion, The Royal Canadian Regiment Battle Group (1 RCR BG) or Task Force 3-06 as it was officially termed. At 1600 hours, 19 August 2006, a small ceremony, the Transfer of Command Authority (TOCA), was taking at Kandahar Airfield (KAF) between Lieutenant-Colonel Hope and Lieutenant-Colonel Omer Lavoie, the CO of TF 3-06. Within hours of the TOCA, before Operation Medusa could even be launched and with portions of his force having only been in theatre for a few weeks, Lavoie was fighting his first major battle.[1]

Reports from locals indicated a continuation of the infiltration of insurgent fighters, as well as new leaders, into the Panjwayi District. More troublesome was the reporting that a large portion of the reinforcements moving into Pashmul were assessed as the more experienced Taliban fighters from out of area who were likely augmented by foreign fighters. They continued to reinforce their defensive positions in Pashmul but also began conducting noticeably more and better coordinated attacks. They demonstrated a large improvement in their use of fire and movement, and their ability to coordinate and concentrate their fire. The insurgents began to conduct almost daily ambushes along major routes targeting ISAF and ANSF elements.

The new TF reacted quickly and pushed out its companies to monitor enemy activity. On 19 August, which was actually Afghan Independence Day, with the TOCA ceremony barely finished, "A" Coy, 1 RCR BG was deployed to the dominating high ground at Ma'Sūm Ghar to observe the enemy. They arrived at approximately 1730–1800 hours and linked up with the ANP, who maintained a presence on the high feature. This activity initiated a prompt response from the enemy. At approximately 1845 hours the Taliban launched a major assault against the Bazar-e-Panjwayi District Centre. "I had not anticipated having my first command combat experience within hours of transfer of command authority," conceded Lavoie.[2]

But he had no say in the matter as an estimated 300–500 insurgents, armed with small arms and RPGs and using disciplined section fire and movement, began to manoeuvre to overrun the ANP and "A" Coy positions on Ma'Sūm Ghar. Their assault entailed dismounted coordinated attacks from the three different directions. Lavoie recalled, "The first thing that struck me about ground combat was the absolute chaos that reigned when the bullets started flying." He explained, "Within a span of a few hours, 'A' Coy came under attack at night by an enemy that seriously outnumbered them." And true to combat throughout the ages "everything that could have possibly gone wrong, seemed to; the enemy was attacking from all directions, serious confusion occurred with regard to identifying friendly Afghan Security Forces in the same battle, ammunition was beginning to run low, there was only one way on to and off of the position, numerous vehicles broke down or got stuck and one LAV III even rolled over."[3]

Major Mike Wright, the OC of "A" Coy, actually a PPCLI sub-unit seconded to the 1 RCR BG for rotation 3-06, arrived at Ma'Sūm Ghar and abruptly noticed that the ground was dramatically different from what he had expected from his map study. He promptly set about positioning his FOO and sent his company battle captain, Captain Mike Leaky, to site his LAV III on the south side of the position to protect their rear flank. "At about 1845, I sat down to do my confirmatory orders," recalled Wright, "and then that's when we got into RPG problems." The first of many RPG rockets sailed three feet over his vehicle. "And basically that's when the contact began," he explained.[4]

On arrival, Captain Leaky and several of the platoon commanders quickly liaised with the ANP and ANA who had observation posts (OPs) and machine gun positions set up on the various peaks on Ma'Sūm Ghar and began incorporating themselves into the defensive plan. Warrant Officer Michael Jackson remembered, "The platoon commander just got off the hill and up to the OC when the rockets started flying and the RPGs hit all over the perimeter." Jackson reacted immediately. "I placed one section on the east side of the hill we were occupying and another section on the west side with me ... We brought the C-6 [GPMG] up into the saddle and we started engaging about 20–30 Taliban on the bottom south side of the hill."[5]

Everyone expected the main threat from the north, the direction of the infamous white schoolhouse. However, the insurgents were infiltrating from every other direction. The enemy was engaged at up to distances of 3,000 metres but they pushed on relentlessly. In the growing darkness, "A" Coy found it increasingly difficult to differentiate the enemy that was swarming over the adjacent peaks as they overran the ANP observations posts from the ANP who were quickly abandoning their positions. Major Wright, the OC, described, "Our first clue that the ANP no longer had control of the high feature was when we had the RPGs fired at us."[6]

The situation became tenuous. "We had to get our guys off the hill out of contact," described Jackson. "And then the section on the west side got pinned down by enemy fire." Jackson manoeuvred another section up on his the western flank to provide suppressing fire to allow his soldiers, who were pinned down, to withdraw from the death trap they found themselves in. But the enemy had arrived in force. "Every time we popped our heads up to take well aimed shots, the bullets were ricocheting off the rocks in front of us," explained Jackson. "But we had to get that section down because we saw enemy off to the far west flank and Taliban off on the far east flank and then we started seeing flashes of light to our north. So it was very apparent that they were starting to surround us."[7]

By that time the ANP were streaming down from their positions on the high ground, abandoning the dominating terrain to the Taliban.

"Next thing you know," pronounced Jackson, "we started taking rocket fire from that OP." The company LAVs were now hammering the mountain tops with their cannon and machine guns, allowing Jackson some manoeuvre space. Under the blistering fire of the LAVs, he was able to pull his sections off the hill. A C-9 light machine gunner and Jackson were the last two men off the position. "We suppressed the Taliban to a point where we could get off," he reminisced.[8]

Concurrently, Captain Leaky was fighting a war of his own. Leaky and his LAV were singularly positioned on the south flank to protect the rear of the company position in the unlikely event of enemy infiltration from the south. It soon proved to be one of the Taliban's primary assault routes as they attempted to skirt the mountain and approach from the rear using the grape fields as a covered approach. "A lot of fire came in our direction and I couldn't identify an enemy so I jockeyed forward to get a better position of observation," declared Leakey. For the next three hours Leakey and his crew fought back the Taliban, who engaged them from two grape hangers and the surrounding fields. The enemy, in formed groups of up to 15 fighters, attempted no less than five times to conduct section attacks on Leaky's lone position. Fortuitously, he fought back each attempt.[9]

The assaulting insurgents proved to be nothing less than tenacious. The fight had lasted over three hours when "A" Coy pulled off the feature in darkness and under contact. "You just couldn't tell who was who," revealed Jackson, "and we were very lucky we didn't have any blue on blue [casualties]."[10] Moreover, "A" Coy could no longer secure their position and were running low on ammunition. Major Wright decided to pull back to more defensible ground about three kilometres outside of Bazar-e-Panjwayi to resupply and regroup. At that point the "Quick Reaction Force" (QRF) platoon from Patrol Base Wilson met up with the sub-unit and delivered the much-needed ammunition. Once they were "bombed-up" Lieutenant-Colonel Lavoie ordered "A" Coy to link up with the ANA and retake Ma'Sūm Ghar.

As Wright led his company back along the main route to the objective they ran into multiple ambushes. To add to their troubles, as the rear platoon turned onto the dirt road leading to the mountain, one of its LAVs tipped over, prompting a recovery operation under enemy fire. Concurrently, the OC was receiving information from higher headquarters, gleaned from various technical means, that there were a number of Taliban platoon-sized units deploying in the vicinity of their intended location. Wright became concerned and called the CO. "At this point," Wright recalled, "I said, you know we're basically doing an advance to contact by night into the enemy's terrain.[11] Lavoie relented and directed Wright to pull back to the outskirts of Bazar-e-Panjwayi and form a leaguer for the last few remaining hours of darkness.

In the end, the defence of Ma'Sūm Ghar, which represented the outer perimeter of the district centre, had blunted the attack against the ANP headquarters (HQ) inside Bazar-e-Panjwayi. Coalition battle-damage assessment indicated that approximately 80–100 insurgents had been killed. In fact, local security forces recovered the bodies of at least 37 insurgents, a remarkable feat in itself as the Taliban were always meticulous in policing the battlefield so as not to leave any indication of their losses.

In the aftermath of the attack, events had once again reinforced that the Taliban build-up in the Panjwayi/Pashmul region represented a significant threat to ISAF and ANSF movement along Highway 1. The build-up also presented a formidable obstacle to the establishment of the Kandahar ADZ. Not surprisingly, the upcoming Operation Medusa took on an even greater importance.

Having beaten off the Taliban attack, Lavoie now focused his task force on the approaching mission. However, he still had to ensure that the Taliban were kept in check until he was ready to launch Operation Medusa. Between 22–29 August, Lavoie's task force undertook deterrence patrolling to prevent the Taliban from attacking the district centre. Meanwhile, the planning for Operation Medusa was in its final stages.

Lavoie gave formal orders for Operation Medusa on 27 August 2006. "TF Kandahar [designation of TF 3-06 for the operation]," he detailed, "will secure Pashmul in order to set the conditions for the Kandahar ADZ."[12] The CO outlined that he intended to achieve his mission by denying the enemy freedom of movement or action within the Panjwayi-Zhari-Kandahar-Arghandab greenbelt, which had historically served as a significant sanctuary and transit route in past efforts to seize Kandahar City.

The operation was to be a joint ANSF/ISAF initiative, with the ANSF leading wherever possible. Lavoie explained, "The key to success of this operation lies in our ability to match our strengths against enemy weaknesses in order to constantly disrupt his decision cycle and prevent his C2 [command and control] assets from being able to react to our manoeuvre." He directed that the BG would "make maximum use of joint fires, ISR, EW, [electronic warfare] superior direct firepower capability, mobility and C2 to dominate the three dimensional battle space and overwhelm an enemy capable of operating on only one plane of the battlefield."

Lieutenant-Colonel Lavoie planned on tricking the enemy into believing that a major assault on their lines of communication, as well as on their command-and-control nodes, was imminent. He hoped to achieve that by advancing aggressively from east to west on two separate axes with two respective balanced company group (Coy Gp) teams — one advancing from the north and the other from the south. The plan was premised on the notion that once the Taliban understood that their critical vulnerabilities were being threatened by a major ground force they would mass to defend themselves. That would allow ISAF assets to destroy them using precision fire from CAS, aviation, and artillery.

Lavoie and his BG were originally given eight days to clear the objective. The precursor to the operation began on 1 September, when the Coy Gps moved to their waiting areas, located close to their objectives, and conducted battle procedure in preparation for their opening roles. "B" and "C" Coy Gps were responsible for conducting feints north and south of Pashmul respectively, with a view to drawing the enemy out of their defensive positions. Concurrently, "A" Coy Gp was to isolate Bazar-e-Panjwayi in order to provide flank protection to "C" Coy Gp due to the nature of the threat and terrain. If successful in their actions, the enemy would be pummelled and annihilated by precision guided munitions and indirect fire.[13]

The following day, 2 September 2006, at 0530 hours, TF Kandahar manoeuvre elements deployed into their battle positions centered on enemy objectives in Panjwayi/Pashmul. "C" Coy, under command of Major Matthew Sprague, was responsible for seizing Ma'Sūm Ghar. Lavoie wanted to ensure he took possession of the high ground first, namely the Ma'Sūm Ghar feature, from which he could dominate the area by both observation and fire. "C" Coy did so without incident, arriving on the objective at 0600 hours, which was the intended "H-Hour."[14] Captain Rob Carey remembered, "When we rolled in there we caught the enemy completely by surprise." He described how his platoon immediately took up fire positions and engaged the enemy across the river. "Our LAVs rolled in there and we probably killed about 10 guys right off the bat ... They were building their defensive positions and those LAVs just chewed them right up."[15]

By 0615 hours, Sprague radioed his higher HQ and declared that there was "no pattern of life across the river."[16] By 0630 hours air and artillery assets began to engage targets of opportunity. Inexplicably, Brigade HQ cancelled a planned air strike on a number of known or suspected Taliban command-and-control nodes. Nonetheless, "C" Coy Gp joined the shooting gallery and engaged Taliban defensive positions from their commanding position on the heights of Ma'Sūm Ghar.

As the operation began to unravel the initial impression was deceiving. Lieutenant-Colonel Lavoie received reports that there were no Taliban in Panjwayi. In addition, civilian women and children, reassured by the ANSF/ISAF presence, remained in their compounds. In Pashmul, coalition situation reports (SITREPs) indicated that "23 of 25 TB [Taliban] in cemetery were KIA [killed in action]."[17] TF Kandahar HQ noted, "Since operations have commenced, 80 TB have been detained by ANSF forces and it is assessed that 250 insurgents in the Objective area have been killed or wounded." Despite these reports, the CO held his manoeuvre elements firm in their current Battle Positions. According to the Brigade plan the enemy was to be pummelled for another 48 hours.

Although outnumbered, Lieutenant-Colonel Lavoie was not concerned. "Even though they [Taliban] had a 6–1 manpower ratio over us," revealed Lavoie, "they could never bring their superiority in numbers to bear or concentrate their force." Quite simply, Lavoie exploited the electronic spectrum. Through his ISTAR capability he could often adjust to Taliban manoeuvres and react in such a way so as to disrupt their decision cycle. For instance, through unmanned aerial vehicles (UAVs) he could watch them manoeuvre to form an ambush, "which

I could then counteract by firing hellfire missiles into that ambush site, followed by artillery." Furthermore, through their situational dominance the coalition forces could detect the enemy massing on mountaintops, or moving to a specific road junction, and before the Taliban even reached their destination they would be bombarded with artillery. Consequently, they "were able to keep just ahead of their decision cycle and prevent them from getting within ours and as a result we could normally outmanoeuvre them."[18]

At this point, not surprisingly, the CO was confident with the progress of the operation. Having the enemy basically fixed within the coalition cordon, albeit with a thin, loose noose, ISAF and the ANSF could hammer the Taliban into submission. "Once that area was seized and the enemy was hemmed in from the north and south, [the intent was] to continue to engage the enemy for the next three days with primarily offensive air support, as well as artillery and direct fire, in order to, from my perspective, determine where the enemy actually was, and to degrade the enemy's ability to fight before we actually committed the main force into the attack," explained Lavoie.[19]

Degrading the enemy with fires became the responsibility of Major Greg Ivey, the battery commander who was collocated with the BG CO. "The indirect fire mission for the Pashmul area was essentially to neutralize and destroy as much of the command and control and suspected strong points of the Taliban as possible," explained Major Ivey. "So, we deployed the four M-777 155mm howitzers north of the Pashmul area along with the brigade assets, which included basically 24 and 7, around the clock, close air support for the first three or four days." He elaborated, "We had approximately 10 hours of attack helicopters by day and five hours by night. We deployed three FOO parties in and around the Pashmul area to essentially conduct preparatory fires to basically set the conditions for the battle group to move onto the objective on foot or in LAVs ... At 0600 hours on 2 September, we had two FOO parties south along the Ma'Sūm Ghar mountain range, one FOO party in the north, each affiliated with their respective rifle company in the area. And it was a shock and awe start." Ivey described, "When we rolled on at H-hour the battery opened up on positions to the south and the FOO parties were pushing close air support assets forward, just pounding away at whatever strong points we had identified."[20]

The ground chosen for the initial move was prescient. "The BG commander and I were sitting up on the hill and we had a perfect view of the entire area, so between him and I we would identify what targets we wanted to actually hit and what effect we wanted to achieve," recalled the battery commander. "We balanced that with what the manoeuvre commanders at the company level wanted to achieve in their little area ... So between myself and my FOO parties that's basically what we did. And, it was a non-stop sound and light show. And it was amazing." Major Ivey revealed, "We fired a quick stab and then we fired 1,600 rounds of 155mm from the battery alone. I can't even imagine or think of the last time that would have been done that as an army ... We had over 150 CAS sorties just to support the opening phase. And, an equal number of attack aviation sorties." Ivey assessed, "Between the three FOO parties, as well as my own party, it was around the clock. And the whole intent of it was, reminiscent of World War I/World War II tactics, simply to pound the crap out of the enemy on the north side of the river. It was for the most part bottom up driven fire planning. It was basically [hit] what you could see on the ground."[21]

The effects of the initial bombardment and direct-fire attack on the enemy positions were not lost on the soldiers. "The air campaign during Operation Medusa was awesome," remembered one participant. "We had ringside seats on the ridge at Ma'Sūm Ghar and we would watch the aircraft come in and drop their ordnance and blow the shit out of the Taliban ... it was great." He added, "You would see five Taliban run into a grape-drying hut that was impervious to the direct fire weapons and we would call in an air strike and the aircraft would drop a 1,000 pound bomb that would take out the entire building."[22]

Some described the events as a "shooting gallery." Lavoie recalled, "You would just sit up there [on Ma'Sūm Ghar] and you'd be taking your turn in the turret with the 25mm cannon ... In the first 48 hours of the engagement you never had more than one or two of my LAVs at a span that were not engaged with targets."[23]

The plan was going better than expected. The battery commander acknowledged, "We were able to achieve some surprise because the

Taliban did not know where the next crump was going to go or at what time. So most missions opened up and fired for effect, three to 10 rounds per gun." Concerns about the terrain and the robust mud compounds and buildings were mitigated by the fire plan. Major Ivey explained the heavy salvos were designed "obviously for surprise to catch these guys [enemy] up and about before they had a chance to get down into their trenches and their defensive works, but secondly because the mud walls and trenches are thick — anywhere from three to four feet wide at the bottom and they stand 15–20 feet tall. Therefore, you need a good weight of fire to actually crack through these buildings." He added:

> Due to the nature of the close ground, a 155mm round could easily be sucked up in a compound and the effects would not go out beyond it. So what we tried to do was at least mass fires with a half-decent volume of fire to do that. So superimposed onto these missions, the forward air controllers in the same FOO parties would also be controlling the close air support. So as an example, on the eastern side of Objective Rugby one of the FOO parties might have been trying to neutralize or destroy a compound from which we had received EW [electronic warfare] hits. Simultaneously, my other FOO party that was with me in the south could have been controlling two A-10s [Thunderbolt aircraft] and dropping laser-guided bombs onto a similar type of target two kilometres off to the northwest, in Objective Rugby west. Concurrently, we would be using all our available assets to strafe the canals and fire through the thick trees. We would also try to assess the actual battle damage assessment as best we could.[24]

But the wild card remained — where exactly was the enemy? "We really did not have a good idea as to where each of the enemy positions were," conceded Major Ivey. "In training it was very easy to see the figure-11 targets and vehicles and you knew where the left of arc and right of arc were, but I'll tell you, out there [Panjwayi] you didn't see people moving around very much. And when they did, we got on them right away, either with 25mm cannon or with indirect fire."[25]

Despite the provocation, or more probably as a direct result of the intimidating firepower, the Taliban chose not to show any reaction. The absence of any major enemy action or movement created an impression of weakness in the eyes of some coalition leadership. The question became: were the enemy already destroyed or effectively weakened? Or where the Taliban just refusing to take the bait, choosing instead to remain safely hunkered down in their prepared positions?

The MNB Commander, Brigadier-General Fraser, visited the forward Coy Gp in the early afternoon of 2 September, at Ma'Sūm Ghar, and decided that the TF would cross the Arghandab River without delay. "C" Coy Gp had already cleared two lanes from their battle positions on Ma'Sūm Ghar, down to the river. They had taken their bulldozers and ploughed two widely dispersed lanes through the grape fields directly to the river flood plain. With those preparations already in place, at 1400 hours the officer commanding (OC) "C" Coy, his engineer detachment, and a security platoon conducted a reconnaissance (recce) to map out possible crossing points.

"I drove up and down the river bed," recalled Sprague, "still thinking we would have two and a half days of bombardment in accordance with the plan so we could do this [assault river crossing] in a deliberate fashion … No one had been down to the river yet — it was not an issue of getting across, but rather getting a foothold on the other side." Sprague further explained, "The enemy side of the river was steep and heavily covered with brush."[26] It became evident that the only clear flat-crossing point was alongside the main road, directly in line with the famous white school complex in the village of Bayenzi that had caused so much grief for TF Orion a month prior, during the desperate combat of 3 August.[27]

"This was the ground the enemy had chosen to defend," acknowledged Brigadier-General Fraser. "[Objective] Rugby [the approximate area around the school complex] was where we assessed that the Taliban wanted us to fight them. That was their main battleground." The brigade commander elaborated, "Their whole defence was structured to have us

coming across the Arghandab River in the south and fight into Rugby ...
And the schoolhouse was the area in the centre, where there were big killing fields to the east and the north."[28] Surprisingly, that also became the
ground ISAF agreed to fight on.

Fraser ordered Sprague to push the security platoon across the river
and leave them on the far side. "I was unhappy with this," acknowledged
Sprague, since they would be isolated in terrain that the coalition neither
controlled, nor fully understood exactly where or how large an enemy
force was located there. The CO, Lieutenant-Colonel Lavoie, was successful in arguing that there was no tactical advantage to leaving a platoon exposed on the edge of enemy territory and they were withdrawn
as darkness fell.

But the BG was not out of the woods yet. More surprises were in
the offing.

CHAPTER FIVE:

Chaos at the White Schoolhouse

MAJOR SPRAGUE WAS RELIEVED when he was given permission to pull his platoon back to the friendly side of the river. However, his relief was short-lived. During the middle of the night both the CO and OC were completely surprised by the ensuing orders from Brigadier-General Fraser. "At midnight I heard we had to cross the river," recalled a perplexed Major Sprague.[1] The brigade commander ordered the TF to conduct an assault river crossing at 0200 hours. Hard words were exchanged and Lavoie pushed back, concerned at the change in plan and lack of preparation. Despite an apparently successful day of bombardment and cursory reconnaissance of the river, there were just too many unknowns. The crossing point was not marked; they had no data on the flow rate or depth of the river; and, most importantly, they had little information on the enemy's disposition. Faced with those obstacles, Fraser relented and agreed to a first-light attack.

Despite the change in H-Hour the pressure to attack sooner than later was tangible. The MNB operations officer, Lieutenant-Colonel Shane Schreiber, explained, "On 2 September, which was D-day, we spent most of the day pounding known Taliban positions in Objective Rugby and Cricket, especially a big bunch of buildings that became known as the white school. We pounded them for a good 12 hours. I mean it was a fire power demonstration."[2]

That impression was widespread and conclusions about the effectiveness of the bombardment were drawn and reinforced by local perception.

"We had reports that the Taliban were actually leaving," acknowledged Schreiber. "That they were actually running away ... The locals said yeah, they're [Taliban fighters] abandoning their positions, they're leaving ... And the enemy could get out, because they had covered routes in and out of the area."[3]

The prospect of the large concentration of Taliban fighters escaping unscathed concerned senior NATO commanders. Lieutenant-Colonel Schreiber revealed:

> When Major-General Benjamin Freakley [ISAF Deputy-Commander for Security] heard that the enemy may be escaping he said "They're leaving, you're letting them out of the bag." That was his big fear is that the Taliban would get out of the bag and we'd have to fight them again later. So, he said, "The Taliban are leaving so you have to get in there and get after them." Lieutenant-General Richards [the ISAF commander] agreed with him, so we started to get a significant amount of pressure to get in there and to actually find out what was going on in Objective Rugby.[4]

The pressure was redirected to the battle group. "We [MNB] directed Omer [CO 1 RCR BG] to do the crossing earlier," asserted Schreiber. "We wanted him to go under the cover of darkness on the night of 2/3 September, [but] he wanted to wait until the morning of 3 September." The MNB operations officer acknowledged, "In the end, there was a bit of a compromise made. We originally said 0100 hours, Omer said 0600 hours, so we settled at 0400 hours." However, Schreiber revealed that "in reality, by the time he started his crossing it was 0600 hours."[5]

Nonetheless, based on the pushed timelines, "C" Coy Gp had no choice but to use the only existing crossing point leading into the killing fields that the brigade commander had previously described. On 3 September 2006, at 0445 hours, engineer elements crept out to clear the route that the infantry was to use. Efforts were slightly delayed because of the darkness and the necessity of waiting for the air-support package.

Sprague recalled, "I gave combat team orders on the fly over the radio." But he lamented that "half of the combat team wasn't even with me at 0545 hours." The orders for the attack were basically "single file, order of march and follow me," stated the OC.[6] At 0620 hours, the leading elements of "C" Coy Gp crossed the Arghandab River under cover of A-10 "Thunderbolt" and B2 fighter bomber aircraft.[7]

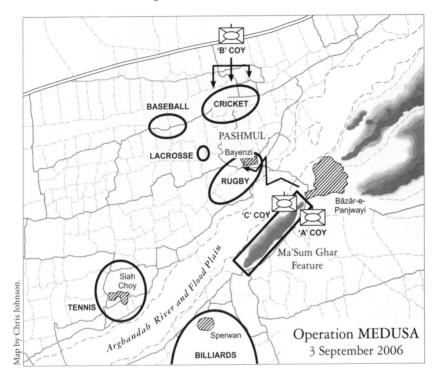

Map by Chris Johnson.

Operation MEDUSA
3 September 2006

They were also supported by overwhelming artillery support. The battery commander, Major Ivey, stated, "We conducted a deliberate fire plan to get the guys across. The 'C' Coy FOO was Captain Dan Matheson and he went across with Charles Company." Ivey and the CO, as well as an anchor OP, remained on the dominating ground of Ma'Sūm Ghar.

> We had close air support basically for a 24-hour period
> starting 2 September, basically prepping the enemy side
> of the obstacle [Arghandab River] … We pounded the
> enemy position and then we pushed fires back into

the enemy depth, into what we would have expected was their supporting positions … At H-hour on the 3 September, Captain Matheson used suppressant fires on that bank just to get the guys shaken out from their battle position on Ma'Sūm Ghar onto the Arghandab River. It was also used to suppress the enemy while they were actually crossing and conducting the actual breach … Once they gained lodgment on the far side or on the north side of the river, Captain Matheson pushed the fires back into the Taliban depth. He also had close air support at the same time to strike even deeper, probably about 1,000 metres or so.[8]

Under cover of the overwhelming fire the mission proceeded smoothly. "We crossed and got into a descent defensive posture and established a good foothold," explained Sprague. "We were in a half circle with 8 Platoon facing West, 7 Platoon facing North, the ANA and their American EMT team facing North-East and the engineer, Zettlemeyer, and bulldozer and other support elements in the flat area behind us." [9]

To Lieutenant Jeremy Hiltz, the 8 Platoon commander, the whole scene upon crossing was eerie — the landscape was completely still. "We knew deep down inside, we knew they [Taliban] were there … but it's still quiet and there's no indication that anything's wrong, except for guys are looking at each other, there's that feeling."[10] He added, "The guys were definitely on high, high alert and heightened senses, but to that point we weren't seeing any type of activity or any, anything that would indicate that there was any issues."[11]

To get through to the suspected enemy positions "C" Coy Gp had to traverse a farmer's field that had been ploughed out. To make things worse it had a series of ditches and berms that had to be breached. The ditches, in the middle of a huge marijuana field, were approximately three to four feet deep and about eight feet wide. The engineers took the dirt from the berms and simply filled in the ditches to make crossing points. Sprague sent 8 Platoon, and dismounted to clear some buildings on his left flank. He sent the ANA, also dismounted, off to his right flank to keep an eye on the main road. Shortly before 0800 hours he sent 7 Platoon, mounted in their LAV IIIs, straight up the middle through the breach. "Initially," reported Sprague, "we all thought this is too easy."[12]

Despite the initial progress, some had concerns. "Unfortunately, there was a lot of confusion due to lack of significant orders and being pushed forward quickly," asserted Lieutenant Hiltz. "It was my impression when we stepped across the river that we were to just push over onto the far side and secure it. And then all of a sudden it seemed like we were breaching and starting to push into Objective Rugby, significantly the white bunker, white school complex." Hiltz described, "The engineers were able to make their first breach and then they pushed forward with the bulldozers and started the breaching of the canal itself ... They pushed through a second breach through the berm, down in between my Bravo and Charlie call signs [LAV IIIs] and then we again secured that ... the initial order was that 7 Platoon would go through and with the engineers move in on the white school and bunker. They [7 Platoon] went across the canal and basically fanned out four abreast and advanced on the white school."[13]

Captain Derek Wessan, the 7 Platoon commander, gave a quick set of orders to his platoon, who then moved through the engineer's breach and shook out into a battle line consisting of three 7 Platoon, or call sign (C/S) 31, LAV IIIs (i.e., C/Ss 31A, B, C), and an engineer LAV C/S E32D. In addition, there was a light utility vehicle wheel (LUVW), the German manufactured *Gelaendenwagon*, more commonly referred to as the "G" Wagon, in which the platoon second-in-command (2IC) rode. The G-Wagon, C/S 31W, was jokingly referred to as 31 "woof" since that "was the last noise you'd hear as the vehicle was engulfed in flames."[14]

Although the landscape was still as 7 Platoon worked its way through the final breach, the enemy had not been idle. A variety of surveillance assets, as well as the deployed troops themselves, began to report on Taliban activities in the depth of the enemy position that began to respond to the initial stages of "C" Coy Gp's advance. Groups of 10–15 insurgents were reported moving about and occupying three-to-five-man ambush positions overlooking IEDs planted on the route leading to the enemy position. These targets were continuously engaged. In fact,

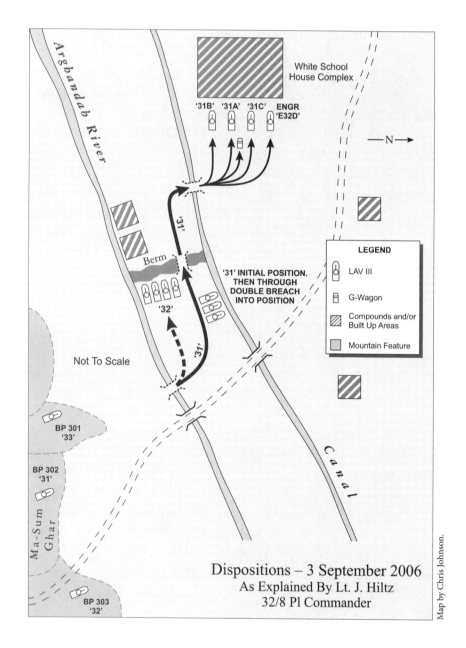

White School House Complex

'31B' '31A' '31C' ENGR 'E32D'

—N→

Argbandab River

Berm

'31'

'31' INITIAL POSITION.
THEN THROUGH
DOUBLE BREACH
INTO POSITION

'32'

'31'

Not To Scale

LEGEND

LAV III

G-Wagon

Compounds and/or
Built Up Areas

Mountain Feature

BP 301
'33'

BP 302
'31'

Ma-Sum Ghar

BP 303
'32'

Canal

Dispositions – 3 September 2006
As Explained By Lt. J. Hiltz
32/8 Pl Commander

Map by Chris Johnson.

it became clear that there were a lot of enemy and that "C" Coy Gp had stirred up a hornet's nest.

As 7 Platoon emerged on the other side of the breach, they found themselves in the middle of a marijuana field. There was an unnatural calm as the 7 Platoon LAVs pushed through the gap and took up an extended line facing the white schoolhouse complex, approximately 50 metres away. The Platoon second-in-command, Warrant Officer Rick Nolan, pulled up in his G-Wagon and took up his position.

The enemy displayed remarkable fire discipline. They allowed the Canadians to approach extremely close before they opened fire. But when they did it had a devastating effect. "It was dead quiet," remembered Master-Corporal Allan Johnson, commanding the LAV III C/S 31A. Then he saw an enemy jump up on a roof and "all hell broke loose."[15] Corporal Justin Young recalled, "We pulled up through the breach and then when we shook out to extended line and then the rockets started flying."[16] Lieutenant Hiltz stated, "When 31 was approximately 50 metres from the white school, a pen flare went off and then it was a very concentrated, very rehearsed and well, well-organized ambush, almost 360 degrees around us."[17]

Regardless of how the ambush was triggered, what is certain is that without warning 7 Platoon was enveloped in fire from three directions. "The entire area just lit up," described Johnson. "We were taking fire from at least two sides, maybe three, with everything they [enemy] had."[18]

Charles Company combat team was now ensnared in a horseshoe ambush. Worse off was 7 Platoon, which found itself in the very heart of the avalanche of enemy fire. Master-Corporal Justin O'Neil, the engineer, field section 2IC, recalled,

> We crossed the Arghandab River, or dried riverbed, and put in two breaches heading towards the white school complex. My section was on the left-hand side of the breach behind the D6 dozer. The other engineer call sign, E32 Delta [C/S E32D], was behind the Zettlemeyer on the right side of the breach. I was in the air-crew sentry hatch and had a pretty good view of the area. We

pushed in towards the white school and then all hell broke loose — RPGs, small-arms fire, everything. Then all the India call signs [infantry — "C" Coy Gp] started working their way up. We started pulling our heavy equipment guys out just because they were sitting there on the ground with no guns. I was watching C/S E32D starting to extract his section when I saw his LAV take a hit — a rocket in the turret.[19]

The engineer LAV, E32D, was the first vehicle casualty, hit by a munitions from an RPG or 82mm recoilless rifle. The heat round slammed into the turret ring of the LAV, spraying lethal shards of shrapnel everywhere in the interior. Sergeant Shane Stachnik, who was standing in the rear hatch, died instantly from a severed artery. Amazingly, the troop commander who was in the turret took only a minor wound with some shrapnel in the shoulder and beside him his gunner escaped completely unscathed. Both were leaning forward to look through their gun sights when the round came whistling in, missing them by inches. The explosion also destroyed the radios, so neither the OC nor the 7 Platoon commander knew what had happened to their engineer.

Shortly thereafter, Warrant Officer Nolan's G-Wagon suffered a catastrophic hit. A RPG slammed into the unarmoured vehicle, penetrating the passenger windshield. "We rolled up, crossed the river, waited till the engineers formed a breach," recalled the driver, Corporal Sean Teal. "Then we rolled through the breach with the LUVW behind the centre … I was the driver, Warrant Officer Nolan was my front passenger, the doc [platoon medic] was behind him and the interpreter was right behind me." He continued:

> We sat there for a few minutes, we were joking around about, you know, kind of ironic that you're rolling into battle in a weed [marijuana] field, but immediately after that just a flash followed by just a big burst of heat, the big crush. And then everything went black. I was out the

door. Grabbed my rifle. I didn't know at the time if anybody else was okay because I'm the tactical combat casualty guy as well. And I took a gander to the left, I yelled over to Corporal Reid that we got hit, which was obvious. I provided a small bit of suppressive fire and then got behind the G-Wagon. The door swung open, the doc, the doc jumped out of the G-Wagon. I pulled him behind the vehicle because he was really stunned. The interpreter fell out, landing on his head. And the warrant [Nolan] didn't come out. That's when I pretty much assumed that either he's probably unconscious because I knew that it had hit his side of the vehicle, actually it came through the windshield directly in front of him. I told the doc to stay put, then I went around the passenger side, pushed the door open. I took some pretty good enemy fire while doing so. The warrant was lying unconscious. There was a fire in the vehicle so I put it out, pulled him out, and dragged him behind the vehicle. The doc couldn't give me a hand at that time because he was still pretty concussed. I made a quick assessment based on the severe wounds that he [Nolan] was a PRI 4 [priority 4 casualty, i.e., dead]. I went back and grabbed the warrant's weapon. I then butt stroked the doc and he snapped out of his daze. He then confirmed the warrant was a PRI 4, which I had already told him.[20]

Corporal Richard Furoy, the medic or "doc," was sitting directly behind Nolan. "Everything in the world came down on us and then, whoomp, the G-Wagon went black," recalled Furoy. "I sort of lost consciousness ... [but] I could still feel the spray of gunfire; I could feel the concussion of the rounds inside my chest, but I couldn't hear anything."[21]

Everywhere individual battles of heroism and courage were played out in isolated dramas throughout the battlefield, which had become a cauldron of fire. Sergeant Scott Fawcett was surveying the ground from the rear sentry hatch of his LAV III, C/S 31C, when he ordered his driver to stop abreast of the other platoon vehicles as they approached to within 30–50 metres of the white school complex. Fawcett witnessed E32D and the G-Wagon get hammered by rocket fire in quick succession. He quickly reported the events to Captain Wessan, who was riding in C/S 31C since his own LAV was non-serviceable.

Fawcett turned his attention to the G-Wagon, which was a blackened and smoking wreck by then. Behind it he could see Corporal Teal desperately signalling for help. Without hesitation Fawcett told Private Mike O'Rourke and Corporal Jason Funnel to follow him and they exited the relative safety of their LAV and sprinted into the inferno outside. "Running through the marijuana towards the G-Wagon, the noise of the guns was deafening and the enemy fire was shredding the tall plants. It was raining marijuana on the sprinting soldiers."[22] Private O'Rourke recalled, "As we dismounted it was just like out of the movies, you hear the whizzes of the bullets and the RPGs — just wicked crazy sounds."[23]

Once they reached the G-Wagon the gravity of the situation became clear. O'Rourke and Funnel began applying first aid to Furoy and the interpreter, who were both seriously hurt. Meanwhile, Fawcett and Teal focused on engaging the enemy to relieve some of the pressure. Realizing the tenuous position they were in, Sergeant Fawcett ordered his men to transport the wounded back to the LAV while he and Teal continued to provide covering fire. O'Rourke and Funnel twice traversed the bullet-swept field to evacuate the wounded, an act of bravery for which they received the Medal of Military Valour.

Meanwhile, the entire company was hammered by small arms and RPG fire. Even the Zettlemeyer front-end loader to the rear of the fighting was quickly hit with an enemy 82mm recoilless rifle and put out of action. Every weapon available was fired in return, but no one could see their antagonists. Corporal Gary Reid insisted, "You couldn't see them. There was minimal movement but lots of rounds." He added, "There was small-arms fire coming from everywhere, RPGs, everything that they had they threw at us. I think we spotted two guys and the rest was all spec[ulative] fire."[24]

"The whole time," lamented Private O'Rourke, "you couldn't see a thing. You couldn't see any movement, anything."[25] He added, "So the whole chain of command is just yelling put down some suppressive fire. And I'm a C9 [LMG] gunner and so far every time I've had to use my C-9 it's crapped out on me. Every time." A despondent O'Rourke bemoaned, "It's a horrible feeling when you're in battle and you're popping off a few rounds and then you get a dead gun. A horrible feeling."[26]

Even the gunners in the hulking LAV IIIs had difficulty. The marijuana plants were so high that the gunners in the turrets failed to see any targets. Nonetheless, the barrels of the 25mm chain guns soon glowed with heat as suppressive fire was rained down on the suspected enemy positions. Many of the guns jammed due to the incessant firing and the pintle-mounted machine guns soon ran short of ammunition.

At one point in the desperate battle the main gun of the LAV commanded by Master-Corporal Sean Niefer jammed after firing just a few rounds. Realizing the plight of his fellow soldiers caught in the open, Niefer stood up in his hatch, fully exposed, and began to lay down a barrage of fire using the pintle-mounted machine gun in the turret. To many who witnessed his selfless act of bravery to support those around him, his total disregard for the bullets and shrapnel whizzing through the air became representative of the vicious battle "C" Coy Gp found itself in. Clearly, there was no lack of courage.[27]

At the same time, 8 Platoon was fighting through a group of buildings on the left flank. Master-Corporal Ward Engley's section dismounted to secure a large ditch. "All of a sudden the whole world exploded around us," recalled Engley. RPGs, mortars, small arms, and machine-gun fire, seemingly coming from all directions, slashed the air. Nevertheless, the 1 RCR soldiers made their way to clear the complex array of compounds and buildings. They were required to go back and clear out buildings that had already been cleaned out because the compounds had so many passages and tunnels that the enemy could use their greater knowledge of the terrain to re-infiltrate the areas that had already been cleared out.

Adding to the problems of the 8 Platoon soldiers were malfunctioning grenades. Instead, the troops used their M72 66mm rocket launchers to clear buildings. A door would be kicked in and the M72 tube punched into the room and fired. The effect of the blast and concussion gave the soldiers bursting into the room the necessary edge.

By that time the platoon commander, Lieutenant Hiltz, had dismounted and ran down the left flank to check on the progress of his soldiers. He explained, "I ran down to my left flank, the south side, and I pushed forward. I'd had several soldiers within my two section actually slightly concussed, knocked out by RPGs. They figure that they took no less than 10 RPGs in their position alone that hit the buildings that they were around ... They were able to push forward and hold that position."[28] Nonetheless, the incoming fire was heavy and Hiltz attempted to get assistance from 9 Platoon, which was deployed in a firebase on Ma'Sūm Ghar. He threw white smoke hoping that it would serve as a reference point. Unfortunately, from 8 Platoon's vantage point it was hard to tell whether the call for support fire was having any effect.

Concurrently, the ANA element assigned to the assault was also heavily engaged. The ANA were apparently fearless. Initially trailing behind "C" Coy Gp, as soon as the Taliban ambush erupted the ANA troops "ran past us with their kit firing on the run," described Sergeant Donovan Crawford with admiration. "They raced up without hesitation."[29] Lieutenant Ray Corby asserted, "They [ANA] [were] quick, aggressive and eager."[30] Lieutenant Hiltz affirmed, "It was actually quite awesome to see that and it brought me back to grips with exactly what I was required to do. I needed to continue to push the platoon out and cover off and allow 7 Platoon the ability to pull back."[31]

By that time Sergeant Fawcett and his men had retrieved the dead and wounded occupants of the G-Wagon and returned to their LAV. But Charles Coy Gp could not seem to catch a break. As the platoon began to withdraw from the trap it found itself in, the driver of C/S 31B backed into a ditch. Like a beached whale, the LAV was stranded and unable to move. Half suspended, its wheels were spinning wildly in the air. The crippled LAV became a preferred target for the enemy and RPG rounds sailed in, a number of them finding the target. The back door was hit, rendering it useless. Other rounds smacked into the vehicle — its armour saving those inside.

C/S 31C quickly came to the support of the stricken vehicle. Broadside to the enemy fire, the crew commander directed the soldiers in the back to take cover in the ditch, which provided greater protection, until they were able to evacuate the troops from the back of the stranded LAV. In the ditch, one soldier "could hear the 'ting ting ting' as small-arms fire hit the LAV and he felt the vehicle rock as first one and then a second RPG slammed into the rear hatch area."[32]

The occupants of the stranded LAV now had to make their exit through the escape hatch since the back ramp of the LAV had been rendered inoperable by the RPG strikes. One at a time, the soldiers made the dash to the closest piece of shelter and provided covering fire for the next individual to run the enemy's gauntlet of fire. Once all were safely out they loaded into C/S 31C, however, space soon became an issue. "There was no room because we had approximately 12 to 13 guys in the back of a LAV III, which is in my eyes a miracle," commented Private O'Rourke. "I don't know how we fit so many people back there. But thank God for it."[33] Unfortunately, due to the lack of space, Sergeant Fawcett and Corporal Fields were on their own and had to make their way out of the death trap dismounted. Due to the circumstances, the body of the platoon warrant was initially left behind with the stranded LAV III in the ditch.

The situation continued to spiral out of control. It seemed that luck was simply not with "C" Coy Gp. A French Mirage Jet zoomed in to deliver badly needed air support but for some inexplicable reason the 1,000 pound GPS guided bomb went off-course and landed 20 feet from Major Sprague and his men. Sprague recalled, "The entire firefight stopped as everyone watched this bomb bounce towards us … I thought, we're fucked now." Corporal Rodney Grubb reminisced, "In the middle of all this chaos, we see this big, black fuck-off bomb coming towards us … it was like a big, black steel football. It hit the ground and bounced and bounced and bounced." Grubb hit the ground and concluded, "Okay, we're done."[34] Fortuitously, the bomb never went off.[35]

As the recovery of vehicles continued the firefight intensified and "C" Coy Gp continued to be plagued by mishaps. The tow vehicle recovering the LUVW missed the breach and the G-Wagon fell into the ditch. After two and a half hours of attempting to recover it, Sprague made the call to blow-in-place (BIP) in order to deny any advantage to the enemy. One positive development occurred when the engineer LAV, C/S E32D, which had been struck in the opening salvo of the ambush, was also in the process of being recovered. As they began the recovery effort the unconscious driver came to and was able to drive the damaged vehicle out of the trap.

Major Matthew Sprague realized that there was not much more he could do so he directed more fire forward and calmly organized the withdrawal of his forces, ensuring that neither casualties nor disabled vehicles were left behind. Warrant Officer Frank Mellish established a casualty collection point (CCP) behind the now disabled Zettlemeyer in a hollow in the ground. When Mellish discovered that the body of his best friend was still in the stranded vehicle he grabbed Private Will Cushley to help him retrieve the corpse. Before they could move an 82mm recoilless rifle round slammed into Zettlemeyer, spraying the area with hot molten shrapnel.

Lieutenant Hiltz recalled, "I was running in to check on my C-6 [GPMG] team, and I vividly remember an RPG round heading directly towards me. And as I went down into the ditch where the C6 team was, it actually flew over my head." Hiltz remembered turning around and looking back and witnessing the tragedy about to unfold. "The round impacted on the Zettelmeyer and essentially the blast rained down right onto the group there," he explained. "It initially looked like everybody was okay but then I realized that there were quite a few of them that were wounded."[36]

Lieutenant Justin Bules, the 2 Platoon commander, stated, "My LAV was about 25 metres in front of the Zettelmeyer and my head was out of the turret and a recoilless rifle round came over my head, hit the Zettelmeyer and spalded."[37] Whether RPG or 82 mm recoilless rifle, the effect was the same; the impact of the round mortally wounded Mellish and Cushley.

On top of Ma'Sūm Ghar a Canadian special operations forces (SOF) combat control team watched the tragedy unfold. "The LAVs were stuck in the field," described one SOF operator. "They were crammed in a little field and they had no mobility ... We saw guys dragging bodies into a CCP and then there was a big explosion and then just guys laying there."[38] Another witness from the SOF team affirmed, "It was one of the most frustrating things I've ever had to watch."[39]

On the ground the situation seemed tenuous. "It was total chaos," opined engineer Warrant Officer Roger Perreault.[40] It had become a fight for survival. As the battle continued to rage, 9 Platoon, located in a firebase position on Ma'Sūm Ghar, was frustrated by their lack of ability to fully support their sister platoons. Captain Carey attested to the feeling of helplessness that C/S 33 experienced. "We just knew that they were under contact, they were in a kill zone and we knew that one of the vehicles had been hit by RPG and that there were casualties, so we just started laying as much fire as we possibly could to their frontage … We had to be careful because there was quite a bit of confusion on the net and they were in the marijuana fields so they couldn't tell where the fire was coming from, they couldn't get a fix on the enemy."[41] Carey confirmed, "There was quite a bit of mayhem on the ground there."[42]

Sergeant Jamie Walsh noted, "After they got hit we tried to engage as best as we could." He emphasized, "We started engaging the schoolhouse and the bunker system right away."[43] But part of the problem was the limited arcs of fire that 9 Platoon possessed. "We couldn't fire at a lot because it would have been shooting right through [C/S] 31 and [C/S] 32's positions," conceded Sergeant Walsh. One of the SOF operators concluded, "The firebase was not far enough to the flank so they didn't have adequate arcs of fire so once across the river, 'C' Coy was on their own."[44]

Nonetheless, once the firebase heard that there were mass casualties "we started to pound everything that we could," stated Sergeant Walsh. "We called in for a reference, so one of the sections threw out white smoke and told us everything east of the white smoke was friendly, everything west was enemy … so we just used the white smoke as a reference point and just started hammering everything, trying to keep their [enemy] heads down to let [C/S] 31 recover their casualties and to be able to pull off the position."[45]

As Charles Coy Gp began its withdrawal, one issue still remained. Someone had to retrieve Warrant Officer Nolan's body. Sergeant John Russell quickly stepped up. "Sergeant Russell pulled forward in his LAV and once he got the go ahead we fired at a rapid rate," described Lieutenant Hiltz. "It was complete mayhem as rounds were going in both directions all around them." The LAV pulled up to the stranded vehicle and Russell and Private Spence dashed out, grabbed Rick Nolan's body, and pulled him back into their LAV. "In a matter of two minutes they were back out and we covered them the whole time," assured Hiltz.[46]

Back at the CCP, Lieutenant Bules had backed up his LAV, lowered the ramp, and began loading as many of the wounded as possible. "We backed up and put the ramp down near the CCP," stated Bules. "I didn't have anyone in the back of my LAV that day so I had just put the back hatches down and we had gone in just with the crew for the battle."[47] By the time Bules was ready to pull out he had 12 soldiers and the bodies of the deceased in his LAV III. He was unable to put his ramp up and he had no chain so "we just pretty much drove out of there with the ramp bouncing up and down every time we hit a bump," recounted Bules. "I just kept telling my driver to go slow and he kept saying we got to get the hell out of here."[48]

Major Sprague turned to his FOO to assist with withdrawal. "When the company commander was prepared to withdraw, Captain Matheson brought in air-burst rounds onto the marijuana fields and the corn fields, probably about 200 to 250 metres out in front of the company's dismounted troops to assist with the extraction," explained Major Ivey. "At the same time, there were buildings in depth that we suspected the Taliban were using to fire RPGs and 82mm recoilless rifles so as best as we could we used hellfire missiles from the attack helicopters, as well as 500 and 1,000 pound laser guided munitions to neutralize those areas." Ivey clarified, "it was a tough slog because it was probably the first time that the FOO had been put in a situation like that where he was with the company commander conducting the fire plan, using the 25mm cannon, controlling artillery at danger close distances under contact and his forward air controller [FAC] in the back [of his LAV] was controlling the aircraft all at the same time. So there was a lot going on."[49]

The withdrawal continued and all of the wounded and dead were pulled from the bloody field of battle. All the stranded vehicles that could not be recovered were "BIP'd" by CAS. "C" Coy Gp then regrouped. "We pushed back into the centre of the riverbed and just leaguered up and basically composed ourselves, and got all the casualties out," stated Master-Corporal O'Neil, "then we pushed back to battle position 302."[50]

The attempted assault on the enemy positions had been costly. The TF suffered four killed and eight wounded. "How more people weren't killed," pondered Sprague, "I don't know."[51] He asserted, "This wasn't some one-hour firefight we were in — we were fucking fighting for our lives, for seven hours."[52] Private Daniel Roasti asked the same question. "I'm convinced someone was watching over us ... The amount of bullets that were flying, I just don't know why some of us are still here."[53]

Once "C" Coy Gp moved back to battle position 302 on Ma'Sūm Ghar "it was basically business as usual for us," commented Major Ivey. He explained:

> The offensive air support plan kept slogging along as intended and that night we had a significant amount of air based on the day's actions, since we now had a pretty good idea where the enemy was. So, the FOO parties basically began trying to destroy as much of those compounds as they could and that happened all throughout the night. And I remember specifically, and I will never, ever forget this — that night just seemed to go on forever because we were on Ma'Sūm Ghar and we kept dropping artillery and bombs anywhere from 1,000 to 3,000 metres from our own location. And the echo of the bombs and the A-10 Thunderbolts and the other aircraft that we had just rang through the entire Arghandab valley. And, you know, we'd try and get to sleep as best we could behind the vehicles and the light from the explosions was so bright that it would go right through your eyelids as you were sleeping. And, you couldn't sleep because you could see the explosions go off because we were up on top looking down into the valley and every strike would just light up the entire valley.[54]

By 1700 hours, 3 September, an intelligence report revealed, "the enemy believe that they are winning, and their morale is assessed as high."

In fact, the Taliban quickly claimed victory following the withdrawal of "C" Coy Gp back to their battle positions on Ma'Sūm Ghar. Moreover, despite the loss of a significant amount of Taliban fighters, the intelligence report concluded that it did not have a demoralizing affect on the remaining Talibes. In fact, the defence of Pashmul became a rallying point for the local Taliban insurgents and they began pushing reinforcements into the area and re-manning many of the abandoned ambush positions.

Lieutenant-Colonel Schreiber, the MNB operations officer, took a stoic stance. "It was either a really good feint or an unfortunate attack. Either way, despite the loss of life, it worked like it had to happen, because it unmasked Taliban positions." He clarified, "So we sucked back, pounded it some more — we spent the remainder of that day pounding the hell out of them [Taliban] and Omer pulled back to set up and to try again the next morning."[55]

"C" Coy Gp regrouped. "We pulled back to the battle position and we began to take stock and to start the healing process and start talking through some of the issues while still maintaining a strong force on the line," explained Lieutenant Hiltz.[56] Major Sprague spoke to the entire sub-unit about the day's activities and then passed on the word that "C" Coy Gp was going back in the next morning to do a feint at approximately 0700 hours, following Bravo company's feint from the north, in an attempt to draw the Taliban out of their defensive positions. Hiltz asserted, "So the plan was that we would get everything ready to go that night. We would take a good night's rest and have a chance to suck back and take a breather and focus on what had happened and then realize that we had a job to get on with."[57]

For many in "C" Coy Gp the prospect of going back into the grinder was daunting. The chaos at the white school complex was still fresh in their memories. Particularly unnerving was the fact that very few actually saw the enemy. In the residual glow of the ongoing bombardment of the enemy positions, the soldiers prepared for another assault at dawn.

CHAPTER SIX:

Tragedy at Dawn

The change in the original plan created a great deal of dissension within the ranks. Many of the participants could not understand why things were "rushed" and why the additional 48 hours of bombardment were not permitted. Retrospectively, they argued that that would have weakened the enemy physically and psychologically, and provided more time to map out the enemy's strength and disposition.[1]

"There seemed to be a rush to get '3' [call sign 3 — 'C' Coy] across the wadi, with no real orders," commented one soldier. Another stated, "We were pushed across the wadi but then what? We weren't even sure what the objective was ... We were going into the unknown."[2] Private Will Needham offered, "We rolled in, drove right into an ambush site, and it was told to us the night before that this grid was basically an ambush site."[3] One soldier quietly concluded, "The enemy was surrounded, cut off and wildly outgunned. We held all the cards, and we played their hand."[4]

Many of the senior NCOs were equally unimpressed. Master Warrant Officer Keith Olstad summarized their overall dissatisfaction. "There was a plan," he stated emotionlessly, "and you only vary from the plan if the enemy influences events ... [the change in plan] was influenced by decisions not by the enemy."[5]

In the aftermath of the failed attempt by Charles Company to secure Objective Rugby the intelligence community underwent serious self-examination to determine what had gone wrong. Was the ferocity and strength of the enemy ambush unexpected? Was it in fact an intelligence failure? The conclusion was a resounding "no." Captain Chris Purdy, the TF intelligence officer revealed:

> We in the intelligence community had a sit-down and we were basically trying to figure out amongst ourselves who had come up with any assessment [regarding the enemy leaving the pocket]. And, an intelligence assessment that stated that the enemy had actually left was not made. I think basically the assessment [to launch early] may have been based on some frustration that we weren't seeing the enemy, yet through sensors on the higher level we [intelligence community] knew that the enemy was there, but legitimately we could not say exactly where they were. And I think it was probably recognized that if we were to go in there and do something it was going to have to be an advance to contact in the first stage. The intelligence community was basically saying that we still know the enemy are there, the assessment is that they're going to stay and fight, especially within the particular vicinity around Bayenzi. They may fold in the surrounding areas, but [Bayenzi/Objective Rugby] was going to be the Taliban's last stand right in that area. And, due to the ground, they really were able to shape us into where we had to cross. The whole area was very canalizing. Again with TF Orion's experience, we knew where they got hit when they tried to come from the south, when they tried to come from the north, and then from the east. So we basically picked a spot where we thought that the engineers could doze, get some LAVs actually rolling across because when TF Orion went across, there were heavy, heavy IEDs on the main routes. So we were adamant that we would not take these main routes because we know that they are just laced with mines and IEDs. We were pretty limited to what spots we could choose to roll a LAV across the river.[6]

Captain Purdy extrapolated, "As far as the intelligence preparation of the battlefield (IPB) goes, it was a combination between brigade intelligence assets, the ASIC [all source intelligence cell] and the battle group ... Originally we thought that the enemy would mass and we'd be able to bomb them for four straight days." However, he quickly added, "The intelligence side never actually said that that was going to be the case. We [intelligence] actually were wondering why we were going ahead with this feint when we were assessing that they [enemy] were probably more likely to draw us in [to their kill zones] ... That's what we were trying to do to them. So we knew it would likely come to a head and then there would be a stalemate."[7]

Another intelligence officer was blunter. "The intelligence was clear!" exclaimed the officer. "The General was clearly informed! And clearly [he] chose to ignore the intelligence." The distraught officer stated, "Intelligence can only advise the commander; that was done, he made the decisions."[8]

In the end, Lieutenant-Colonel Lavoie was never given a reason for the change in plan but he suspected that the initial success, specifically how easily Charles Coy Gp had seized Panjwayi, had created a false impression in the higher headquarters. Originally, "everyone was expecting a real fight, but it never materialized," stated Lavoie. "We rolled through the village unopposed, seized the high features [Ma'Sūm Ghar and Ma'ar Ghar], isolated the village and then started pounding the enemy on the other side," explained the CO. Lavoie believes that the unmitigated victory created the impression that there was an opportunity to exploit.

Regimental Sergeant Major (RSM) Chief Warrant Officer Bob Girouard supported his CO's assessment. "Because there was no return fire from the enemy [on 2 September] the brigade felt that there was not going to be any enemy resistance — that the enemy had dispersed ... Therefore, instead of giving the CO his three days, they wanted him to go in immediately. And from there, basically, is when everything more or less went astray."[9]

"They [Brigade] wanted to rush it through," acknowledged Lavoie, "so I asked what happened to the original timelines." He described how each layer of leadership is continuously pushing for results on the ground. "Consistently higher pushes," noted Lavoie. "They want IO [information operations] successes, and brigade in turn is pushed by NATO HQ [headquarters] for obvious success, however, the calls for greater effort and faster results never come with resources … Since there are not sufficient resources, you must phase the operation, therefore it takes longer."[10] Lavoie later lamented that the worst moment of his tour operationally "was crossing the Arghandab on 3 September and losing four soldiers killed in action despite my gut instinct telling me that conditions were not set and the intelligence picture was not clear and the battle procedure was too compressed/non-existent." He acknowledged, "I said no the first time but the rest is history."[11] A now seasoned Lavoie concluded, "Now, I just say no — I learned my lesson the hard way at the beginning of the operation."[12]

Lavoie's assessment was correct. Brigadier-General Fraser conceded, "I would say there was a tremendous amount of pressure from ISAF to 'get it done!'"[13] However, he disagreed with the soldiers' criticisms. "You don't fight a plan; you fight the enemy guided by a plan … The enemy also has a vote and if you ignore the enemy you will lose."[14] By 2 September Fraser believed the situation was changing and it was an opportune time to attack. In short, he felt there was nothing to be gained by waiting another 48 hours.

"I knew a lot of the enemy were there," Fraser acknowledged. "But, you know, you do two more days of bombardment, how many do you kill? How do you know that? You guess. No matter if you went in on the second, third, fourth, fifth, or sixth, guess what, ladies and gentlemen? It is a difficult thing to cross a river and to go into a main defensive area where the Taliban were waiting and wanted to fight on. It would have been gut-wrenching, whatever day was picked to go across the river."[15]

Lavoie, the CO of TF 3-06, framed it another way. He focused on the limitations of airpower as a key lesson that emerged from the early combat. He explained:

> I sort of kick myself for having to relearn the lesson in regard to airpower because it's something I think every army officer, army soldier knows intuitively, that is, that you cannot win with air power alone. And in the Battle of Pashmul, I just got sucked into it — I probably had an exorbitant dependence on, or overestimation of air power. We dropped thousands of tons of munitions on them in the days before we had to start conducting

the ground operations. But in the end, as we relearned, you just cannot rely on it because until you actually get in there and muck out those fortified defensive positions you just can't be sure. It's a matter of getting those ground forces in there and taking the enemy out. It was hard for us not to get sucked into it because you were sitting on the high ground watching our forces just closing them down with 25 mm cannon fire and the soldiers were seeing just literally hundreds of thousands of tons of bombs being dropped on the objective. You couldn't just help thinking that there was nothing that could survive in there. Well, we found out the hard way that they could. That is a lesson that we probably relearn in every modern battle that we have fought since we started using air power. So, you just can't overestimate the effects of air power on a low tech enemy.[16]

Regardless of the recriminations, one fact remained: the enemy was in Pashmul in force and had to be destroyed. Moreover, it was later revealed that despite the enormous bombardment, the enemy's positions were still intact. Lieutenant Hiltz observed, "The HE [high explosive] was just like a fingernail scratching on a chalkboard, it wasn't really doing much damage."[17] As Lavoie finally concluded, the infantry were simply required to go in and "muck out" the enemy. Therefore, regardless of the debacle of 3 September, the brigade commander ordered the TF to try again the following morning. The plan was to try and draw the enemy out by feinting more to the south, forcing the Taliban to react and leave their fortified positions. Then, as per the original plan, they could be annihilated with air, aviation, and indirect fire.

Reveille for "C" Coy Gp on 4 September was 0530 hours. They were to launch an hour later. They followed their normal routine — ablutions and burning garbage. Then disaster struck. Lieutenant Hiltz remembered vividly:

The boys were eating breakfast, the guys were doing their shift change around and guys were packing their kit up. As was generally our procedure, during daylight hours we would burn our garbage. I'm not quite certain who lit a fire, but one of my members of my platoon lit the fire that morning that was directly behind the OC's vehicle, as well as my right-most vehicle. And then it was approximately about 0515 hours that I remember just vaguely, I remember I was eating a strawberry Pop-Tart, sitting there chatting with one of my section 2 ICs, the vehicle crew commander, talking about how cold it was and we both basically turned to get out of the vehicle as it was time to really pack up our kit, get everything ready, when it was like the 4th of July about 10 metres behind the vehicle. It was the friendly-fire strike by the A-10. I remember jumping back into the vehicle. I remember Master-Corporal Bellamy, the guy who was in the vehicle with me, basically flying into the vehicle. He ended up in the right-hand side of the turret ring. He flew that far from the ramp and he just jumped. He took shrapnel in the back, close to his spine. Private Keegan, who was with me as well, was not hurt and I somehow was not injured. So again, it was my lucky day in that respect. I remember getting out of the vehicle and there was dust everywhere. And I remember running over and we started grabbing guys and getting guys onto people that were more seriously wounded.[18]

"I knew immediately what happened," asserted the OC, Major Sprague. "You can't mistake that noise."[19] The A-10 was called in to attack an enemy position identified by a small fire. When the responding pilot popped-up over Ma'Sūm Ghar, he spotted the burning garbage on Battle Position 301 and became briefly disoriented. Before he realized his error he unleashed a partial burst of deadly fire from his seven barrelled 30mm

Gatling gun, killing former Olympic athlete Private Mark Graham and wounding 35 others, including the "C" Coy Gp OC.[20]

"The first rounds hit about 10 metres behind me," Corporal Jordache Young recalled. "We saw flashes and looked back — it was mass devastation."[21] Sergeant Brent Crellin observed, "There were sparks in the dust, like the sparklers you wave on Canada Day … And then we heard the burp of the gun and then we felt sick."[22]

Captain Rob Carey was briefly disoriented. "I was just up and I heard a burp in my right ear, which was odd because all the A-10s were staying in front of us because we were basically facing north. I heard it in my right ear and I didn't think anything of it and my LAV sergeant, Sergeant Dinsmore, said 32 [8 Platoon] is under contact." Carey assumed the Taliban had attacked. "Shit, they [enemy], snuck in behind us, they got in behind on the mountains — that's the first thought … So we all stood to and jumped into our vehicles."[23] Within minutes the tragic truth sunk in — it was a friendly fire, mass casualty incident.

Major Ivey, the battery commander, explained, "At around 0500 hours the A-10s were still on station. They had probably been working in that area for about two hours already, maybe a little bit more than that … And they had dropped on the north side into Pashmul already. They went back to refuel and came back down to help us out again — the same pilots." Ivey elaborated, "So they had been on the go for about three hours at that time. Captain Matheson and his crew were engaging targets on the north side of the river around where the white school was and some of the other target areas from the morning before. And for whatever reason, the pilots who admittedly came back and said pilot error over the radio afterwards, confused north with south." Ivey noted that it was "a bad time of day, nightfall turning to day" and that the pilot "had been working his butt off flying for us" and he unfortunately "confused the south side with the north side and ended up strafing what he thought was a group of Taliban huddled around a fire." Luckily, the FOO on station was able to get the pilot to abort and stop the second aircraft on-station from doing a follow-on gun run. Ivey explained, "The tactics for the A-10s call for the second aircraft to follow-up and watch for the splash of the shot and pick up where the last aircraft left off … The aircraft were pushed back up into a holding pattern above us — God bless them, those same guys stayed and provided air cover while we did the casualty evacuation. Concurrently, we threw a fairly extensive smoke screen across the river on the north side to at least blind the enemy from seeing what was going on."[24]

But the drama was not yet over. The crisis was on the brink of getting worse. The 155mm guns were about 10–15 kilometres to the north firing their smoke mission. The smoke canisters were flashing up in the air and tumbling down from the south towards the BG position. A stiff wind from the southwest blew the billowing smoke nicely down along the river valley, creating a grey veil through which the enemy could not see. As the wall of smoke built up, the first UH-47 Chinook medium-lift helicopter could be heard in the distance pounding its way to the landing zone for the medical evacuation (MEDEVAC). Inexplicably, it ignored the briefing from the ground control crew and rather than looking for the designated purple smoke, it flew over the position, saw the smoke canister billowing on the north side of the Arghandab River, and made a direct line towards it.

"So you must appreciate," expounded Major Ivey, "that there is a mass casualty scenario under contact on one side of the river and now you've got a Chinook helicopter flying into bad guy country into the line of fire of disbursing smoke canisters … Just to make matters worse." The lumbering Chinook helicopter actually touched down "for about a millisecond and then realized what the hell was going on," described Ivey.[25] The helicopter quickly lifted off and flew around the BG position, finally landing so that the MEDEVAC could be undertaken. Remarkably, the enemy had not reacted at all to the unexpected target of opportunity.

The latest calamity to hit "C" Coy Gp was disastrous. Having lost most of its command structure and almost a third of its strength in the friendly-fire incident, it was now combat ineffective. "Twenty minutes away from an assault river crossing and Omer [Lieutenant-Colonel Lavoie] lost half a company," asserted Brigadier-General Fraser. "We delayed 24 hours but at the end of the day we had to get it done."[26]

Luckily for the rest of the BG and coalition forces assigned to Operation Medusa the opening moves of the operation were not as catastrophic. In the north, "B" Coy was well established. In fact, by the time Charles Company went across on 3 September, "B" Coy had already been in position for a few days. They were pulled out of Forward Operating Base (FOB) Martello two days prior, passing the responsibility of its security to a Dutch sub-unit so that they could deploy to assist in the combat operations, since no other NATO countries provided forces to fight.[27] On 1 September 2006, "B" Coy moved to Patrol Base Wilson (PBW) and established a large leaguer inside the PBW compound. The next day they deployed and established a two kilometre blocking position, from the town of Pasab west to Howz-e Madad, on the south side of Highway 1.

Their task was relatively simple. "We were to give a feint south of the highway to distract the enemy," said Major Geoff Abthorpe, the OC.[28] The CO's intent was for "B" Coy to push across Highway 1 and protect it as well as the BG lines of communication. Lieutenant-Colonel Lavoie also hoped to draw away some of the attention of the Taliban from the south to the north.

"B" Coy was deployed in line, close to the forward edge of their first objective, code name "Cracked Roof," which was a very deep canal and road system that went through Pasab, a small village north of Pashmul. The ground actually favoured The Royals and their LAV IIIs. From their blocking positions the ground lay open for approximately 500–700 metres to Cracked Roof, which represented the Taliban front lines in the north.

Lieutenant Jeff Bell, the 5 Platoon commander, described, "When the operation started we were in a leaguer up to the northeast of Patrol Base Wilson. We launched from there and my platoon was on the far west flank of the company … We were essentially in a blocking position. It was an extended line with the LAVs out in a fairly open position and we had a treeline about 500 metres away that we were watching." Bell added, "We were right in the vicinity of a yellow bunker. We were essentially covering that."[29]

Shortly after "B" Coy moved into their position, they were attacked by two Taliban gunmen who fearlessly opened fire on an entire platoon of LAV III armoured vehicles with nothing more than their AK-47 assault rifles. "It was the most surreal thing," commented an astonished Major Abthorpe. "The two Taliban stood up in the open on a mud wall and started shooting at the LAVs with AKs, nothing else."[30] Lieutenant Bell immediately conducted a hasty attack on the enemy-occupied compound. In support, the 155mm guns fired a salvo of air-burst munitions that abruptly ended the enemy resistance, allowing 5 Platoon to clear the compound. Despite a thorough search only one body was found.

On the night of 2 September, Major Abthorpe also received notice that timings for the operation had changed. "I get the call saying 'Standby, Charles Company is going across. Pass the word,'" revealed an astonished Abthorpe. "'OK,' I thought. 'This is interesting.'"[31] The next morning "B" Coy conducted its feint up and down Cracked Roof, waiting for the outcome of the battle to the south. "The air strikes started to come in," described Lieutenant Bell. "We had A-10s, as well as Apache attack helicopters firing on the yellow bunker and a variety of other buildings that were assessed as enemy ... We also engaged with the LAV 25mm cannons. After the initial strikes, however, we went into a holding pattern." He explained, "It was an effects-based operation and we were now waiting to see what happened down south to set the stage for our manoeuvre."[32]

But no one was prepared for the news they received later in the morning. "They ['C' Coy] crossed over," explained Abthorpe. "We know what happens. They redeploy back south across the river so we go into holy-fuck mode."[33] "B" Coy held their position and waited for orders, which came quickly.

Lieutenant-Colonel Lavoie assigned Major Andrew Lussier and his ISTAR (Intelligence, Surveillance, Target Acquisition, Reconnaissance) squadron, which was roughly a company-sized sub-unit largely made up of personnel from the Royal Canadian Dragoons (RCD), to join "B" Coy and assist with the northern feint. "The next day [4 September] we were set at the start line at first light, I think it was 5:30 a.m.," said Lussier, "and we were all along just south of Highway 1."[34] The CO's intent was for "B" Coy and the ISTAR Squadron to penetrate Cracked Roof to draw the enemy's attention and focus to the north. The soldiers of both sub-units were poised for the attack, ready to assault when, 15 minutes before H-Hr, the command radio net exploded to life. "And that's when we got the news: 'Stop, stop, stop. Charles Company has just been fucking strafed,'" revealed Lussier.[35]

News of the friendly-fire incident hit everyone hard. "That was one of the worst days of my life," recalled Captain Piers Pappin, the 4 Platoon commander. "The 'C' Coy LAV captain came on the radio as the OC so we all knew there was some real shit … We thought they were all dead."[36] Not surprisingly, everything ground to a halt.

For "B" Coy, somewhat dislocated from the BG, time came to a standstill. However, it was a "little bizarre," according to Captain Pappin, who was anchoring the left flank of the blocking position. "It was what I called the phony war of Medusa … We conducted our feint and then we sat on our positions for quite a long time and we didn't see much enemy activity … We knew they were there but there was not a lot of movement."[37]

It seemed to be a stalemate — neither side was ready to make a decisive move. However, during that period the enemy conducted small probing attacks because, as Pappin observed, "they were confused about what we were doing and would do." As a result, "when the insurgents probed we would do a hasty attack, and kill them and then pull back to our original blocking position."[38]

"B" Coy also closed down an enemy supply and reinforcement rat line into Pashmul. "We noticed a route that no one was covering," recounted the 4 Platoon commander, "so we set up an observation post that observed the area and could cover it with fire … We shut it [enemy rat line] down."[39]

The formation flank to the west was also firm. Brigadier-General Fraser had given that task to TF-31, which was a sub-unit from the 1st Battalion, 3rd Special Forces Group (3 SFG) or "Desert Eagles." The unit, under the command of Lieutenant-Colonel Donald Bolduc, was starting its fifth rotation in Afghanistan.[40] The American TF arrived in theatre with the mission of conducting consolidation operations, which meant establishing, maintaining, or regaining control of key populations centres or lines of communication in the regions, districts, or provinces. Major Jamie Hall, the OC of the American SF "C" Coy, which consisted of six Operational Detachment — Alpha (ODA) teams, was responsible for the Kandahar area, therefore, he was assigned to Operation Medusa. Each of his six ODAs also had a 30 man ANA company attached to it.

Fraser had given TF-31 the task of screening the western flank. As such, Major Hall decided to slip into the operational area unseen. He took a 60 mile route through the Registan Desert, braving temperatures of 48°Celcius instead of using the highly congested and targeted Highway 1 and Highway 4 route from the Kandahar Airfield (KAF) through Kandahar City to the Panjwayi. "I wanted to quietly infiltrate the enemy's battlespace before they knew we were coming," explained Major Hall.[41] However, he conceded that "it was like driving across Mars."[42] But in the end, TF-31 arrived in location and deployed along the western flank.

Nonetheless, regardless of the firm grounding to the north and west, because of the friendly-fire incident a pause in operations was required. The 1 RCR BG needed to reorganize and plan out the next steps. The RCR "C" Coy Gp was sent back to the Kandahar Airfield to regroup and say farewell to their dead. They returned to Ma'Sūm Ghar on 6 September 2006, to rejoin the fight. General Rick Hillier, the chief of the Defence Staff (CDS) summed up "C" Coy's resilience:

On that terrible weekend [Labour Day Weekend 2006], they lost a company commander in action, lost a company sergeant-major, lost one out of three platoon commanders, lost all three platoon warrant officers, one wounded, two killed, lost five section commanders out of nine and lost all of the sections' second in command master-corporals — a total of 40-plus wounded and five killed in a 48-hour period. They all stepped. A young sergeant promoted to sergeant last July became the company sergeant-major. Young master-corporals became platoon commanders and platoon second-in-commands. And young soldiers became section commanders and they carried on the operation and the fight against the Taliban that gave NATO such an incredible boost right at the start of the mission. Now, if that's not a Canadian epic ... I don't know what is.[43]

The return of Charles Coy to the battlefield was mirrored by a press release from the NATO Secretary General Japp de Hoop Scheffer who stated, "[there is] a hard fight, a hard battle going on because NATO forces were attempting to exert control in places such as Panjwaii [*sic*] a no-man's land, where nobody has ever been before excepting small and sporadic past forays by very thinly spread coalition forces."[44] He added, "Operation Medusa is accomplishing its task and I can tell you from everything we've seen and heard today, and the commanders we've talked to, the operation itself is going along well ... I would characterize it as a successful operation that has to take its course and it will in the time that's coming."[45]

The NATO secretary general's carefully chosen words veiled the tensions that existed. Despite the rhetoric of the importance of the battle, few NATO nations actually committed troops to the battle. And, those that did had differing views of how the next phase of the battle should unfold.

"Now Omer [CO] was adamant that he didn't want to try it the same way a third time," revealed Schreiber, "and good on him." The MNB operations officer continued, "We agreed, but we were under a whole bunch of pressure from Major-General Freakley that he wanted us to go. He said you still have another company down there, get that company, get it in there and get after them." Schreiber elaborated, "We didn't want to do it hard, we always were going to do it smart, we didn't want to rush into a failure. So we came up with an alternative plan." The BG was going to use three dismounted companies, clearing from the east, move down the canals to get into the area and then clear out the enemy. "Now that, that was still going to be ugly because we're talking about clearing that area by hand to hand combat."[46]

The ISAF commander was not enamoured with the revised slow Canadian approach. Fraser simply stated that they could not risk taking many more casualties because of the national political ramifications. Lieutenant-General Richards refused to accept that rationale and called Fraser's national command. However, in the end, the ISAF commander was forced to relent. Schreiber asserted:

So commander ISAF said okay, you can do it your way, continue with the slow approach and the emphasis on

fire power. He gave us 72 hours to continue to try and
pull apart the Taliban position in Objective Rugby. So
we took the 72 hours. But, commander ISAF was adamant that at the end of the 72 hours he wanted to move
to what he called the decisive phase, which was to attack
and clear Pashmul, and the three objectives Cricket,
Lacrosse and Rugby.[47]

The pressures on Fraser and Lavoie were tangible. "Brigadier-General
Fraser was getting phone calls from Lieutenant-General Richards and
Major-General Freakley on an hourly basis," revealed Lieutenant-Colonel
Schreiber, "saying this is the most important thing NATO's ever done, the
future of NATO rides on this, the future of Afghanistan rides on this." He
assessed, "There was a lot of psychological pressure being put upon Brigadier-
General Fraser and then being transmitted down to poor Omer [Lavoie] to
get this done faster … There was an implied 'don't worry about the casualties, just get in there.'" However, at the same time, Schreiber acknowledged
there was also "a lot of pressure" from Canadian Expeditionary Command
(CEFCOM) headquarters in Ottawa clearly stating that "you can't have any
more casualties, the political situation is precarious."[48]

In the end, Fraser admitted they "got to a stage where in fact I would
say there was a tremendous amount of pressure from ISAF to 'get it
done!'" But he also insisted, "On the other hand, there was a tremendous amount of support from Canada to do the right thing but not to
rush into it." As always, in war there are a myriad of competing demands.
Fraser realized that there was also a culminating point. "How long could
I keep my assembled forces out here in the field?" he pondered. And of
course, the enemy always has a major vote in the affair.

And so, with a myriad of competing pressures, a well-entrenched
and tenacious enemy as well as an impatient chain of command, both
Brigadier-General Fraser and Lieutenant-Colonel Lavoie had to revitalize
Operation Medusa. A new plan was required so the formation and BG
staffs set to work. On their shoulders rested the fate of a nation and apparently an alliance.

CHAPTER SEVEN:

Payback

By the time what was left of Charles Coy returned to Ma'Sūm Ghar, a new battle plan had taken form. First, on 6 September Brigadier-General Fraser requested tanks from General Hillier, the CDS, because his forces were facing a dug-in enemy.[1] Second, the emphasis of Operation Medusa was shifted from the south to the northern flank, onto the shoulders of "B" Coy Group. Up until that time, "B" Coy had largely sat out the action and had only sporadic and limited firefights with Taliban forces. They were now the primary effort.

Before launching the second assault, however, Brigadier-General Fraser had to reform his brigade. First he created Task Force Grizzly, which consisted of the remainder of The RCR "C" Coy Gp combined with an American rifle company and commanded by the American national command element, which became the TF HQ.[2] "Based on the results of our first probe [on 3 September], it became clear that I needed to adjust," explained Fraser, adding that "the enemy had focused on where he thought we were going to cross the Arghandab River from the south." Quite simply, the ground the coalition had attacked "was key terrain tactically for the Taliban and they had reinforced and defended the northern shore of the Arghandab River," with tenacity and resilience.[3]

Fraser elaborated:

> In fact, they actually created a kill zone in the objective
> area we had code-named Rugby. They had designed to

take us either from the east or from the southeast. They were really focused on us coming from the south and a lot of their commanders were in Kandahar, Sperwan Ghar, and along the southern part of the Arghandab River. Sperwan Ghar was an important area because from there they could escape into Helmand Province or into the Reg[istan] Desert, which led to Pakistan. As a result, based on that assessment and the initial moves by TF 3-06, I decided to give Task Force 31 the task to take Sperwan Ghar and once that was accomplished push across the Arghandab River and take Siah Choy. I created Task Force Grizzly to create the impression of force, but more importantly, it was actually a feint — to deceive the Taliban that we were still coming across the Arghandab River from the south. Meanwhile, I shifted TF 3-06 to the north so that they could initiate a deliberate sweep from our Patrol Base [Wilson] in the North clearing our main axis of advance down to the Taliban strongpoint.[4]

Once the redeployment of forces was complete, Fraser ordered Lieutenant-Colonel Lavoie and his BG to deliberately put pressure on the enemy to force the Taliban to react. Instead of the Canadians continuing to move into ground of the enemy's choosing, Fraser wanted to force the Taliban to react to their choice of terrain. Fraser ordered TF-31 to move north into Sperwan Ghar at the same time that 1 RCR BG started moving from the north, clearing towards the Arghandab River. He changed their mission from one of screening the western flank; in essence flank security, to the task of disrupting the Taliban command-and-control node in Sperwan Ghar. Fraser also had British SOF operating in the Registan Desert to interdict any reinforcements coming from, or retreating enemy attempting to escape to Pakistan. His plan was to clear the ground step-by-step and capture or destroy as many Taliban as possible.

The 1 RCR BG commander was in line with Fraser's intent. "With Charles Coy now combat ineffective," Lavoie explained, "I, in concert with supporting arms commanders and my operations officer created a new plan of attack." He directed "B" Coy to spearhead an assault from the north of Pashmul, moving slow and deliberately to the south. He then pushed his other sub-units forward, securing strong points and clearing routes of IEDs and mines. "With all arms working together and under the constant umbrella of air cover," noted the TF 3-06 CO, "my BG [would] advance towards Pashmul and the Arghandab River."[5]

The renewed push was started on 6 September 2006 by "B" Coy when they breached the treeline that marked the divide between friendly and enemy territory. When word finally came to renew operations, "B" Coy was ready. "We sat on the line so long," commented Captain Pappin, "that we had already done rehearsals and talks on how to breach the line ... At night we also did fighting patrols to define the next bound." As a result, "when we got the word," asserted Pappin, "we knew exactly how to do it."[6]

What they did was borrow an ANA bulldozer, with assurances that they would not break it, and with Canadian engineers driving, they created breaches for the LAV III armoured vehicles to push through to support the dismounted infantry. The first obstacle, "Cracked Roof," was easily breached since a "B" Coy fighting patrol had already seized it.

The offensive itself actually began by miscommunication. The "B" Coy OC was at higher headquarters. When battalion headquarters (BHQ) received the report that the "B" Coy fighting patrol had taken Cracked Roof, "someone" at BHQ misunderstood and erroneously told the sub-unit to move to "Cricket," one of the major objectives. The Coy 2IC, not one to waste time, pushed the sub-unit forward with dismounted troops advancing with the LAV IIIs on the flanks providing fire support. Lieutenant Bell recalled, "And then we got the okay to launch. I was on the eastern flank; Captain Piers Pappin was in the centre and Lieutenant Grant MacDonald, C/S 23, was on the western flank." He described, "When we did the actual advance we all sucked in to the centre so that we had more manageable pieces of terrain to cover. We didn't run into too much [resistance], nothing really."

Once the sub-unit reached the obstacle at Cracked Roof, the bulldozer began to cut a swath through the canal so the LAV armoured vehicles could be pushed through. Just as the rifle company was sizing up the next bound, higher headquarters deciphered the messages and quickly told "B" Coy to hold at Cracked Roof.

That night, however, the enemy struck back. "They [Taliban] engaged with essentially everything they had," stated Bell. Nonetheless, the line held and the next day "A" Coy and TF Mohawk, (specifically "A" Coy, 2nd Battalion, 4th Regiment, 10th U.S. Mountain Division, mounted in HUMVEEs), passed through "B" Coy and pushed further south towards Objective Rugby.

Concurrently, TF-31 reached the 3,000 foot mountain dominating Sperwan Ghar. Major Hall's Ground Mobility Vehicles (GMV) and two of his ODAs (331 and 336), as well as their ANA counterparts, cautiously approached the high feature. Several hundred metres from the top the Taliban opened a withering fire. "We walked into a hornet's nest," described one SF operator. "They were waiting for us."[7] Hall stated, "Within 20 minutes of the start we were running out of ammunition." The SF troops pulled back and reconsolidated without suffering any casualties.

However, for the 1 RCR BG to clear Pashmul they needed a secure flank. After the heavy fighting from the previous day, the ANA were reluctant to go back up to attack the hill. However, Major Hall simply stated, "That's bullshit. We came here to do a job, and the Canadians need a secure flank, we're getting up there."[8] The next day, after a resupply of ammunition and some CAS, TF-31 renewed their assault on the strategic hilltop. Despite suffering casualties due to mines and an IED, the American SF soldiers and their ANA counterparts tenaciously forced their way to the top. By that point the Taliban had lost the will to hold it. Just before sunset TF-31 captured the key terrain.

The coalition then owned the vital ground for the whole area. From that position they could observe Sperwan and Siah Choy. Their efforts did not go unnoticed. "That was one of the most profound acts of bravery I've seen since I've been over here," pronounced the MNB operations officer. "About 24 American Special Forces soldiers, reinforced by an American rifle company, and some ANA actually took that feature from about 200 Taliban."[9]

That night the Taliban attempted to retake the hill, resulting in a sustained battle lasting approximately four to five hours. However, close air support, mortar, and artillery fire pummelled the enemy and by the end of the battle the Taliban were forced to stay on the north side of the river. They had given up their attempts to recapture the strategic hilltop, which was the vital ground for the whole area. The MNB headquarters estimated enemy casualties at 200 dead and approximately 300 wounded. Lieutenant-Colonel Schreiber noted that TF-31 had done the disrupt. They had completely dislocated the Taliban from that area."[10]

Captain Chris Purdy, the BG intelligence officer, summarized the action:

> We had a concern that the enemy would try to flank us. And indeed, I think they would have, had TF-31 not been there [in Sperwan — the western flank] ... They inflicted a significant number of kills in that area and that was one of the main enemy command-and-control nodes as well ... They cut off the head while we were dealing with the main body of fighters. And when that command and control started to get a little skewed the enemy decided to suck back.[11]

Meanwhile, TF-42, the U.K. SOF element stationed in Kandahar, were working down in the Registan Desert cutting off enemy supply lines. "We knew," revealed Captain Purdy, "that a large portion of fighters and some weapons were coming up through the rat lines through desert to get into Pashmul. So the Brits were working down there to cut off that resupply line while TF-31 was working on disrupting the enemy command and control."[12] Clearly, every effort was being done to slowly strangle the Taliban forces that were entrenched in the Pashmul area.

In the south, Fraser's deception ploy was being played out. "I used my American National Command Element (NCE) commander as my Task Force Grizzly commander," elaborated Fraser, "because I needed to generate another battle group when I couldn't get one out of NATO." Lieutenant-Colonel Steve Williams jumped at the opportunity. Fraser acknowledged, "Steve Williams was a warrior — a smart determined, aggressive, outstanding individual ... I gave him a bunch of forces and I told him, that's your sector and here's your mission — what I want you to do is to fix the enemy in Objective Rugby, make them think that you are a whole TF and be prepared to exploit on my order."[13] Fraser bluntly told Williams, "I want you to make yourself look like a thousand-man organization, make the Taliban believe you are still Omer Lavoie."[14]

Back in the north the advance continued. "B" Coy had held at Cracked Roof for about 48 hours and conducted a systematic search of the village of Pasab. The sweep was largely uneventful but they did uncover "big wads of cash and explosives."[15] Two days after the start of the offensive, on 8 September, with a proper breach in place, "B" Coy pushed through Cracked Roof and linked up with Mohawk 6, which was now in a forward defensive position. The bulldozers also moved forward and began to create lanes and breaches in the grape fields to be used as run-ups for the LAV IIIs.[16]

Both companies experienced an increase in enemy engagements as they slowly exerted pressure southwards. But the push was on. The operation became a systemic dismantling of the Taliban defensive system. Each night the reconnaissance platoon would move forward in the darkness and define the next objective. After their report orders would be given and the next morning the designated rifle company, preceded by artillery and CAS, would take the next tactical bound and seize their objective. As one objective was secured a passage of lines would be completed and the next assault element would continue the advance. "With all arms working together and under the constant umbrella of air cover," noted the TF 3-06 CO, "my BG advanced towards Pashmul and the Arghandab River."[17]

The 1 RCR BG was hitting its stride. At one point there was a large open field between the advancing Canadians and their objective. "A" Company moved forward and took the intervening anti-tank ditch and held the line, providing a firm foothold and a firebase. Artillery was called in to hammer the objective and "B" Coy surged forward, broke through into the objective, and started to fight through the target area. It became clear that the Taliban had left a rearguard to slow down the attack.

The clearing of objectives seemed just like Cold War training for fighting the Soviets, according to almost everyone who participated.

What simplified matters was the fact that the objective areas were designated military targets, since the entire civilian population had been evicted by the Taliban and the area was turned into a fortified defensive zone. As such, it became an exercise of unrestricted compound clearance. The soldiers would toss grenades into a building or room and then, immediately after the explosion, pour into it and hose it down with fire. Major Lussier acknowledged, "The Taliban did us a big favour; essentially they had kicked out all the civilians ... It made life so much easier for us ... Essentially we just shot and bombed the crap out of these guys for the better part of four or five days while the battle group made their way from the north."[18]

"When the operation commenced, it seemed as if it were a Cold War training exercise," observed Lieutenant-Colonel Lavoie. "There was nothing new in war fighting." He explained:

> We used air to hit deep and close artillery at 300 yards or less. Dismounted infantry rushed in before the smoke cleared and seized the objective. Engineers cleared a route with bulldozers and dealt with IEDs. We pushed LAVs up to support infantry to the next objective and to the next bound. At night we conducted fighting patrols and Reconnaissance Platoon seized the line of departure for the next bound the next day. And much like predecessors in Vietnam who said they had to destroy the village to save it — we had to do the same. Welcome to my world.[19]

In essence, as the operation began to play out it became increasingly "conventional" in nature. Fraser described it as "a conventional duke-it-out fight." He said, "The enemy wanted the ground and had prepared the area well for a defensive battle. In the end, it was all about putting the proper resources into the fight." The brigade commander asserted, "We knew we would win because losing just was not an option."[20]

Major Ivey concurred with the brigade commander's assessment. "We went right back to using conventional ammunition, high explosives," recalled Ivey. "The air burst, we found, was outstanding for neutralizing soldiers that we suspected were hiding under trees, using the shade as concealment or using the thick brush to move back and forth." He articulated, "So we used air burst a lot, as well as 155 mm delay ground burst to pierce through those complexes to get whatever effect we were trying to achieve, which was basically just to kill people and to destroy whatever bunkers they had." Ivey related that they also reverted to using smoke to blind the enemy, screen their movement, and mark targets for CAS.[21]

The choreography of the advance was in keeping with the conventional warfare playbook that most of the senior leaders in the battle group had practiced since joining the army. "What we ended up doing was, hours before the launch of an advance, each of the respective FOO parties with the two lead companies commenced their preparatory fires," explained Major Ivey. "There was no flashes of brilliance — what we wanted to achieve was to destroy as much of the compound structures as we could that we thought were housing enemy OPs or firing positions and neutralize anybody and anything in the objective areas." As a result, higher headquarters pushed the necessary enablers (e.g., CAS, attack aviation, and guns) to the FOO parties so they could pound the Taliban into submission.

Due to the close terrain and bitter resistance, most of the engagement distances were well under the standard "danger close" distances. In fact, the average distance of engagement by CAS with their 500lb laser guided bombs, attack helicopters with hellfire missiles, and the 155 mm artillery was approximately 300–400 metres, according to the battery commander. "There were a number of instances where you could still hear shrapnel flying out behind you," admitted Major Ivey, "but that's the reality of it — there has to be a certain level of acceptable risk in what you want to do and I guess the question is what's riskier, not hitting that building that might house a recoilless rifle or getting the guys down behind some cover and accepting a bit of shrapnel coming back behind you?"[22]

In the end neutralizing the enemy to allow the rifle companies to advance from their line of departure to their immediate objectives was a very slow and deliberate process. During their push forward, the FOOs would drop ordnance in-depth. Once the assaulting troops gained lodgment onto their objectives the process would start over. "The FOO would get up onto a compound with a dismounted laser range finder, a map, and a pair of binoculars and begin preparing the next bound," explained Ivey. "Yeah, World War I tactics." He laughed. "We would just neutralize anything in front of us and then once that fire had been lifted, we would push the infantry through and occupy that ground and secure it. And that's basically how it worked up in the north."[23]

Captain Purdy reinforced the tactics used. "In the north it was overwhelming air power and artillery … We started getting reports that the enemy cannot move when they're being bombarded and this was a real sense of frustration on the part of the Taliban." He described how the enemy indicated in their communications between themselves that "we cannot achieve our objective while we're getting bombarded." Purdy assessed, "Artillery in this first stage of the battle was instrumental. We could not have pushed the Taliban out of that area without artillery." He also stated that by the time "B" Coy started to push south, "we realized that due to the artillery and the ongoing fighting the enemy started to experience some logistical problems … And that was one of the main aims of 'B' Coy pushing down from the north — to sever two of their main supply lines that we had assessed were the wadis and the canals flowing into that area." Purdy concluded, "So, when 'B' Coy actually pushed through they effectively cut the lines of supply coming in to the Taliban."[24]

The BG had developed the winning template for destroying the Taliban — overwhelming firepower followed up with infantry clearing the ground in a very systematic fashion. Major Mike Wright, OC "A" Coy noted, "It was just a matter of leapfrogging companies through a deliberate sort of advance to contact and/or search to the last and final objective."[25]

And the deliberate advance continued as "B" Coy pushed through TF Mohawk and "A" Coy. Despite the noticeable decrease in resistance the advance was still difficult and extremely dangerous. One of the major reasons was the complex terrain. "You can only see down one furrow lane at a time," explained Lieutenant Bell, "and that's if the vines weren't very thick. Therefore, you had to walk every single one of them to call it clear because you can't just look down a row because there could be something stuffed under the vines or at the bottom of an irrigation canal."[26] Sergeant

Normand Godin stated, "In the vine fields a man could sneak up onto you and be within 10 feet of you before you'd have any idea that he was there." He recalled, "One night a guy snuck up and stole the trip flares and left with them. They were about 15 metres from our position."[27]

Equally daunting was the maze of thick-walled mud compounds that resembled impregnable mini-fortresses. "They have compound upon compound upon compound and then there's another compound," stated Lieutenant Hiltz in exasperation. "And there's no significant plan to it, like we do back in North America, where someone comes in and plans a straight road where you could sit down and have a nice firing lane and a cut off … You may get 100 metres and then there's a turn and another compound kind of offset that would cover it … And then to continue to further complicate things, you have the pot fields, which at this time of year were higher than our vehicles, and still very green." Hiltz grumbled:

> We were unable to burn them and we tried using a lot of different methods, from diesel to white phosphorous dropped down on it from mortars and 203 (grenade) rounds. Then you have the vineyards where they grow their grapes. These are, essentially the easiest way for me to describe it is, picture a speed bump and then add about a metre at a minimum to the height of the speed bump and then put about two feet in between them, and they have 100 of them. You have to move through them and clear them because the enemy has the tendency to sit down inside and burrow back into them and then once you push past them they would come out behind you. That was some of their TTPs [tactics, techniques, and procedures]. And then there is the natural foliage. It's very thick, very good cover, and very difficult to see into. And then to top it all off, unfortunately marijuana has a very good heat holding capability, which further exacerbates our thermal capabilities of the LAV. So it's very difficult terrain. To us there doesn't seem to be a set pattern to it at all, but the enemy definitely has a very

good knowledge of the ground and so they're able to move very well in it. It's the most complex terrain I've ever seen. To make it even worse, at any point in time when you start to make routes you kick up dust that is like talcum powder. It's moon dust. It's about a foot deep and it's very easy for someone to throw something in and to hide it quite easily without the ground looking disturbed. It causes a lot of visibility issues and it clogs up a lot of your weapon systems and equipment.[28]

Lieutenant Bell concurred with his peer about the complexity of the terrain.

You had to make sure that you were in your own compound because all the compounds were inter-joined, so what we would determine as being one compound in planning could, in actuality, have a door that goes into another compound that is the objective of another platoon ... But it's hard because the guys just keep going — push, push, push and all of a sudden we've gone too far and we're in someone else's AO [area of operation] and we have to pull back out ... So that was the hardest thing, just keeping everybody on track, on line and on target with regard to which objectives to go to and which ones to hold back. It was very easy to get sucked in and to just keep going.[29]

There were other problems as well. "The doors were a lot smaller than we were use to," recalled Bell. "A guy with full kit, especially me with the radio, fitting through some of the doors was a bit of a gong show ... We would make our own doors whenever possible because of the booby-trap threat. And even then, using the engineers it would take a couple of blocks of C4 explosives."[30]

The Canadians eventually developed a system and began to cut through the Taliban defensive network. However, they did meet their match in one building: The soldiers conducted their drills and launched into the interior. Within seconds they all came running out in disarray, screaming. The grenades had disrupted a large hornet's nest and they had all been stung. "The Taliban couldn't touch them," laughed Pappin, "but the hornets, or 'Talibees,' were a different matter."[31]

The effect of the systematic BG approach, particularly the incessant pounding by CAS and artillery, was clearly being felt by the Taliban. Casualties were mounting. "There were 80 guys killed in one day," professed Major Lussier, the OC of the ISTAR Coy. "We saw it. We watched it. So, this isn't speculation here." He explained it was a function of "people [Taliban] making mistakes because they're exhausted and stressed." He noted, "We killed a lot of people, you know, we killed a lot of Taliban. And they're just not set up to take a couple of hundred casualties. They're not set up to evacuate them. They're not set up to look after those kind of wounded." As a result, "they just fell apart. And so that was part of the disruption task."[32]

And so, from 6–10 September, the brigade just kept squeezing the Taliban in Pashmul with the BG pushing from north to south, TF Grizzly pounding the enemy from the south, and TF-31 pressuring the enemy from the south west. On 10 September 2006, "B" Coy Gp seized the northern half of Objective Cricket, setting the conditions for Mohawk 6 to move through and capture the southern portion of Objective Cricket the following day. Throughout, TF Grizzly conducted feints to the south to fix the enemy on Objective Rugby. "TF Grizzly was doing a great job keeping the enemy preoccupied in the south while TF 3-06 just cleared down from the north," lauded the Brigade Commander. "Intelligence was telling us, despite the attack and heavy bombardments we were actually seeing fighters who were risking staying in place," revealed Fraser. Nonetheless, he conceded, "The [enemy] command and control was still very effective and still pressing very hard for the fighters to keep on going, even though they were taking a pounding."[33]

Meanwhile, as the operation unfolded, TF-31 remained heavily engaged in Sperwan Ghar in a fight that lasted over three days. Despite severe opposition, TF-31 was prevailing. "The enemy was just dumping on them," described Fraser, adding that "the Taliban [in this location] were coming across the intervening ground in convoys

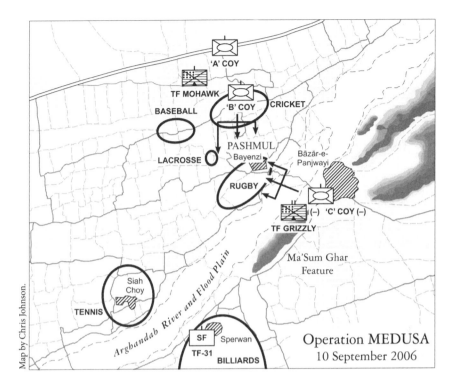

Map by Chris Johnson.

of trucks, dumping off five to 10 guys from each truck, all who just unloaded and attacked TF-31's position … It became a turkey shoot. In one night, I think they killed between 100 to 200 Taliban, it was a phenomenal shoot."[34]

At the same time, TF Grizzly was also meeting with success. Because of the changing dynamic on the battlefield, "we made the decision to press really hard," explained Fraser. He added:

> I mean, it's a feeling in a battle — you can feel the battle when you got the enemy. It's something you cannot teach, you just got to know when to push. Our forces got to that stage. You read the intelligence; you read what the soldiers were doing on the field; and then you just realize it — okay, it's time to push. And we went out there and we pushed because the enemy was starting to pull back, even though we were not in any great strength there.[35]

On 11 September 2006, with Objective Cricket captured and the engineers beginning to improve the routes for better manoeuvre, Brigadier-General Fraser pushed TF Grizzly, with the remainder of "C" Coy, north across the across Arghandab River. "So I said, okay, we got something really big in Siah Choy and in Sperwan Ghar, and there is little pressure coming out of the main stronghold, so I pushed TF 3-06 to get down and take our main objective, which we called Rugby," he explained. "At the same time I told TF Grizzly to get across the Arghandab River get into the eastern side of Rugby and roll up the Taliban position from the flank, realizing that the Taliban would then collapse."[36]

As always, the plan did not unravel quite so easily. TF Grizzly struggled to get across the river. Reinforced with ANP they finally managed to gain a foothold. The MNB Commander then pressed the TF commander to get "Charles" Company (minus), supported by elements of ISTAR [intelligence, surveillance, target acquisition, reconnaissance] squadron, across the river. That too was done against "medium" enemy resistance. Once TF Grizzly gained lodgement into the enemy trench line, Fraser ordered, "TF 3-06 to push hard and link up with TF Grizzly because once we had the momentum going and the Taliban started to fall back, I just wanted to keep the pressure on."[37]

By 12 September, Mohawk 6 had pushed onto Objective Lacrosse. Concurrently, "A" Coy, 1 RCR BG, was preparing to move onto the eastern portion of Objective Rugby. The enemy seemed to be dissipating. The troops found well-constructed entrenchments but they were abandoned. "It looked like they were prepared for a fight," explained Major Geoff Abthorpe, "B" Coy Commander, "but I think over the last few days they lost their gumption to fight and they pulled out before we showed up."[38]

By 13 September NATO estimated that they controlled 65 percent of the objective territory.[39] Coalition intelligence assessed that the insurgents in the Panjwayi/Zhari area had withdrawn west or had stored their weapons and remained in the region. Those fighters not from the area had exfiltrated west along the Arghandab River valley or through Arghandab District to the north. The following day, 14 September, at first light, Mohawk 6 seized Objective Rugby West. They met no enemy resistance.

Brigadier-General Fraser explained, "At that stage of the game, we had great pressure on the enemy — we were coming from the north, from the south and from the southeast." He elaborated:

> We had three task forces that moved in with significant pressure. Lieutenant-Colonel Lavoie and his 1RCR BG linked up with TF Grizzly, which was pushing towards them from the southeast to the northwest. Meanwhile, the moment Sperwan Ghar was secured by Task Force 31, I ordered them to push to Siah Choy. We thought we were going to have a huge fight in Siah Choy based on our experience and the Taliban tenacity at Sperwan Ghar, which was just staggering. As a result, I told the other two Task Forces to just stand by because the main effort that morning was going to be Task Force 31 and their push to Siah Choy. I allotted them priority on artillery, aviation, and everything else.[40]

Remarkably, TF-31 seized Siah Choy without firing a shot. The Taliban had fled. At that point, Fraser pushed his brigade to exploit — he ordered all to move into Phase 3 of Operation Medusa.

"I received word that morning that we took the town without a shot," recalled Fraser. "Nobody was there, therefore, at that point we moved into exploitation ... Amazingly, it's hard to exploit, it's hard to get troops to take more risk. Once you get soldiers going at a certain speed, to get them to change that speed and exploit is difficult." He added, "You read about it in the books and you think, how hard can that be? But it is. I went out and I talked to the commander of TF 3-06 and said now is the time to get all your forces and exploit — that means you take more risks but you don't take more chances or become reckless about the risks you accept." Fraser concluded, "Now you have the enemy on the run and now is the time to take the ground."[41]

And TF 3-06 did exactly that. They seized the ground from the Taliban. "The village of Bayenzi, the home of the infamous white school complex, was the final objective, called Rugby," explained Lieutenant-Colonel Omer Lavoie. He divided it up into company sized components assigned as follows: Rugby Centre ["B" Coy], Rugby East ["A" Coy] and Rugby West [Mohawk 6]. "So when we did the final assault, we just came down the new road and cut off to the east," he described. "Recce Platoon went in the night before to clear and secure the line of departure for 'A' Coy because they were the first company to be passed through." He revealed, "Unknowingly, they had actually secured the enemy objective because the maps were a bit off. So we linked up with Recce Platoon in the morning and found we were actually on the eastern part of objective rugby and I had 'A' Coy start to clear through it." Lavoie recalled:

> It took about four to five hours to clear the eastern part of the objective and it was a classical infantry ground slogging clearance. Shotguns were used to take the hinges off the doors; the doors were kicked in; grenades were tossed in and once they exploded the troops went in spraying the room with machine-gun fire. Then they searched for IEDs and weapons. We found a lot of IED making devices and lots of weapons on Rugby East. We also had to clear the wells. Often you'd throw a grenade down a well and get a secondary explosion because there were RPGs and munitions stored at the bottom and in holes dug into the sides of the well walls. "A" Coy cleared through until 1200 hours and then Bravo Coy passed through and cleared through Rugby Centre. Because their objective was bigger and more complex, it took them a bit longer to do — until almost last light. At first light I pushed my American company [Mohawk 6] through and the entire objective was secured.[42]

Concurrent to Mohawk 6 being pushed through to secure the remaining vestiges of Objective Rugby, Charles Company assaulted across the Arghandab River and attacked Objective Rugby from the southeast. "We established a line just north of the school, and then all of a sudden we start seeing LAV antennas to the north," explained Lieutenant Wessan. "It was crazy. And that was it. Rugby was secure and everything was good to go."[43] So in the end, "C" Coy secured the Taliban stronghold that had punished them dearly.

To Brigadier-General Fraser that was important. "And I wanted TF 3-06 to take that ground because of what they lost there," he stated. "They took some heavy casualties and I mean for them, there was psychological value in that terrain … In fact, I was there when Charles Company actually took it and I was so happy that they were the ones who went across and seized the ground — I thought, 'you took it, no one else did, you guys did it' and that was another reason why I assigned them to TF Grizzly in the south — this was important for that company because it came at a high cost."[44]

Once they had captured the ground the scale of the enemy preparation became fully apparent. "They had extensive fortifications," remembered Captain Pappin, "bunkers, loopholes in thick walls and buildings, and some bunkers were built in the courtyards of mosques."[45] Lieutenant Hiltz explained,

> I was able to get a good look at the actual position itself and everything seemed to indicate that the enemy had prepared fairly significant defensive systems oriented to cover down to the south … Everything seemed to point towards the fact that they were defending in that direction with many lay back positions. And on one occasion I was able to actually see one of the positions before the engineers blew the entrances to one of the bunker systems … As a bunker system with approximately four feet of earth over top of it, a steel I-beam-reinforced roof and the actual interior of it was almost done similar to the crack filling on a wall in a house … It was done smooth and it could have held anywhere from 15 to 25 personnel. They were able to move into that bunker with pretty much impunity through a ditch system,

essentially an irrigation system that was actually ringed
with trees, which would have concealed them ... And
again, they were low enough that it would have given
them cover, so they would have been able to pull back
into the bunker unmolested ... In essence, there was
quite a significant amount of trench system and bunker
systems that they had built.[46]

The extent of the fortifications once again raised the question of how
"C" Coy had managed to escape from the Taliban killing fields with as few
casualties as they suffered on 3 September. Sergeant Dinsmore verbal-
ized what many inwardly thought, "You wonder how we didn't lose more
men actually from seeing this side of the Arghandab River now."[47]

In the end, the assault on the Taliban stronghold in Pashmul was
successful. Lavoie later revealed that the best moment of his tour was the
seizure of Objective Rugby.[48] "The Taliban didn't think we would attack
from the north," surmised Lavoie, "because the ground was impassable
and no one had done that before." He explained that a clever deception
in the south and the use of bulldozers to plough lanes through grape
vineyards and marijuana fields to make lanes for the LAV IIIs, as well as
"B" Company's utilization of the ground in conjunction with overwhelming fire from artillery and CAS at "danger close" range, overcame any and
all opposition.[49] But for how long?

CHAPTER EIGHT:

Declaring Victory

With the taking of Objective Rugby the combat phase of Operation Medusa was over. In the end, Fraser assessed, "after all that pressure, after all that time, the enemy just collapsed and they went to ground."[1] The brigade commander declared that the conditions for TF 3-06 to move from Phase 3 (exploitation) to Phase 4 (reconstruction), namely the creation of a secured area of operations in the Pashmul District, was at hand.

Once again, a phased approach was taken. In fact, a three-stage plan was developed. The first stage entailed restoring security through the visible employment of ANSF throughout the area with RC(S) forces in support. It was also to be the commencement of an enduring ANA/ANP presence in the Pashmul/Panjwayi area. The next stage called for resettlement. In coordination with the Disaster Management Committee and key district leaders, as well as UN and appropriate civil agencies, ISAF forces were earmarked to assist with the return of the civilian population to the area. Finally, the third and last stage of the reconstruction phase of Operation Medusa was the development piece where the larger and more enduring projects targeted for long-term development could take place. After all, Brigadier-General Fraser had pronounced that the end state to Operation Medusa would be achieved when "the people of Afghanistan have freedom of movement along Highway 1, the villagers of Pashmul and greater Zhari have returned to their villages and the Taliban have been denied freedom of action in the vicinity of the Kandahar ADZ."[2]

By 15 September 2006, the various TFs began pushing their presence further out from their original objective areas. Although there were no enemy engagements, there were locals observed fleeing the area, which normally portends no good fortune. However, in this case no combat ensued. Moreover, the Government of Afghanistan and ISAF began radio and television broadcasts to encourage locals to return to their homes, explaining that the fighting had stopped. By 16 September some of the TFs, such as Mohawk 6, were redeployed to the Kandahar Airfield (KAF). The next day, 1 RCR BG began to rotate its companies through KAF for rest and refit, maintaining two company groups on security and clearance operations in their area of responsibility.

It seemed that by 17 September 2006, Operation Medusa, aside from the non-kinetic Phase 4 reconstruction phase, was over. It appeared that the ISAF Multinational Brigade, but particularly the 1 RCR BG that bore the brunt of the fighting in the Pashmul area, had indeed defeated the Taliban. The cost, however, was not inconsequential. In total, the Canadians had five killed and approximately 40 wounded. The fact that Canada bore the brunt of the fighting was not hard to notice. One reporter noted, "Canadians are getting killed at a rate five times the average for NATO and U.S. forces in Afghanistan, where Canada's soldiers have suffered more than one-quarter of the combat deaths in Afghanistan [in 2006].[3]

The victory, however, was hailed as a monumental success. A NATO statement was swiftly broadcast announcing the victory:

> NATO launched its largest-ever combat operation, against a well-prepared and determined enemy. It was fought to the southwest of Kandahar City, in the Panshwaye [sic] and Zhari Districts. It was here that the Taliban filtered in large numbers of insurgents in to first take and then, far more significantly, hold the area. It was a trial of strength that will have a lasting effect both militarily and on the hearts and minds of the Afghan people.[4]

Another NATO missive announced, "The operation has met its initial aims by dealing a severe blow to the leadership and forces of the extremists so that they are no longer a cohesive force and have had to dispense after suffering important losses."[5] A political official was less restrained. He remarked that Operation Medusa "wiped the floor with the Taliban."[6]

Not surprisingly, NATO leadership used the success to push select messages. General James L. Jones, commander of Allied Command Operations cooed, "It has been necessary to fight in this instance to achieve the required effect. Importantly it has proved that NATO will not shirk from taking robust action where necessary and especially given the level of insurgent activity."[7] Similarly, ISAF Commander Lieutenant-General David Richards boasted:

> Operation Medusa has been a significant success and clearly shows the capability that Afghan, NATO and Coalition forces have when they operate together. I always said that I would be robust when necessary, and that is what I have done. The Taliban had no choice but to leave … Having created a secure environment in the area, it is now time for the real work to start. Without security, there can be no reconstruction and development. Without reconstruction and development there can be no long-lasting security.[8]

According to Lieutenant-General Richards Operation Medusa was a key battle against the Taliban insurgency. "If Kandahar fell," he explained, "and it was reasonably close run last year, it did not matter how well the Dutch did in Uruzgan or how well the British did in Helmand. Their two provinces would also, as night followed day, have failed because we would have lost the consent of the Pashtun people because of the totemic importance of Kandahar."[9]

The Afghan government also hailed the success of Operation Medusa. Provincial Governor Assadullah Khalid stated on 17 September 2006, "Six nations fought side by side to inflict significant casualties on the entrenched insurgent forces, who could have avoided this sad loss of life by reconciling with the legitimate Afghan government."[10]

He added, "The ability of the Taliban to stay and fight in groups is finished. The enemy has been crushed."[11] Khalid assessed, "This operation in Panjwai [*sic*] and Zhari is one of very few successes in recent years."[12]

The rather effusive praise from senior NATO and Afghan leadership was echoed by some scholars and analysts. Author Barnett Rubin, a respected global authority on Afghanistan, credited "Canada's military for turning back 'a frontal offensive by the Taliban' in Panjwai [*sic*] last summer and for rescuing Afghanistan from what he considers 'a tipping point.'"[13]

The largely Canadian ground action did not go unheralded by its national command either. The CDS, General Rick Hillier, asserted, "Afghan ministers will tell you that operation [Medusa] saved Afghanistan." He explained, "If Kandahar had been encircled, if Highway 1 had been shut down and if the Panjwai [*sic*] had been held by the Taliban, the government in Kabul would have fallen."[14] Brigadier-General Fraser added, "It was one of the hardest things we've done for a very long time. Canada led the operation, NATO's biggest one ever, and successfully defeated the Taliban in this area. Canada did what was right and the cost was not insignificant."[15]

In more private settings, the MNB commander was more unrestrained. "The ISAF commander was ecstatic," Fraser revealed. "He [Richards] just could not believe what we were able to accomplish … He was very enthusiastic, I mean psychologically, what our troops did was impressive. They saved the city of Kandahar, arguably saved the country and they saved the alliance. They proved that NATO could fight as a coalition."[16] The MNB commander concluded, "We defeated the Taliban with only five of our casualties [killed]. Then the Taliban tried to bug out one night. Not many made it out. We saved the city, and in so doing, [we] saved the country."[17] Lieutenant-General Mike Gauthier, commander of Canadian Expeditionary Command (CEFCOM), believes that Operation Medusa and follow-on operations signalled a major success in Kandahar. He bluntly elaborated: "Kandahar City did not fall; the Taliban heartland was lost by the enemy; the Taliban were unable to maintain momentum in the winter; and the capacity of the ANA was increased."[18]

NATO's initial assessment claimed 512 Taliban were killed and 136 captured.[19] Lieutenant-Colonel Schreiber stated, "It is a conservative estimate that the Taliban suffered 1,500 casualties (1,000 wounded, 500 dead)."[20] Brigadier-General Fraser's assessment was similar. "We think we probably killed about 300 to 400 and captured 136, which includes the death of approximately five senior commanders on the ground. That's a significant defeat, the worst defeat the Taliban ever experienced in probably 40 years, according to the Afghan Minister of Defence."[21]

The effects of Operation Medusa seemed impressive. Brigadier-General Hayfield, the ISAF Chief of Operations, proclaimed, "Operation Medusa was a huge success."[22] Similarly, media reported, "Medusa was, in military terms, a roaring success. The enemy was routed and more than 1,000 insurgents were killed, giving what British and NATO commanders call 'psychological ascendancy' over the Taliban."[23] Moreover, British Brigadier-General Richard Nugee boasted, "Casualties from roadside bombs and suicide attacks have fallen from 245 in September 2006 to 29 for the first two weeks of November and soldiers in Panjwayi have started an $8m reconstruction drive."[24]

The assessment, however, is subjective. The local Afghans had a completely different perspective. "The bombing and the fighting destroyed our mosque, our homes and our vineyards," said one farmer. "The Taliban are gone, but so is most everything else."[25] Haji Abdullah Shah stated, "The cause of the fighting was the Taliban, but with the bombing NATO made big mistakes ... They killed our children, they killed our families. Every canal is collapsed. Every field needs water. We don't have enough food."[26] Abdul Hai lamented, "We have only dirt, nothing else."[27]

Similarly, the long-term impact is more difficult to assess. The Taliban attempt at concentrating and holding ground was convincingly defeated. However, being an adaptive and clever foe, they analyzed their recent defeat and quickly concluded their future survival and success depended on an asymmetric approach to fighting the ANSF and coalition forces. This knowledge made them a far more significant threat and effective insurgent force. Brigadier-General Fraser explained:

So when the enemy left we knew we had won this fight. However, we also realized that they would evolve. We knew the enemy would go back, they would go to ground for a bit [disperse and regroup in safe areas] and that they would do an after action review, after which they would come back at us in a far more sophisticated and dangerous way. They always do, they always adapt. The only question we had was how long was it going to take them to replace their leaders and how long was it going to take for them to come back at us again and what form would it take? When they did come back at us, they did so very quickly. They hit us with suicide attacks, IEDs, and ambushes. So was it a surprise? No. Are they more dangerous now? Yes.[28]

An official Canadian report agreed. "It is expected that the kinetic effects of OP Medusa will be transitory," it stated. "The TB [Taliban] has demonstrated that they are adept at infiltrating fighters into the region and it is expected that enemy force numbers will be replenished in the coming months. Consequently, there is no belief that the TB movement has been defeated in Kandahar Province, nor in RC(S) ... Ironically, there is some unofficial suggestion that the TB will enter into a more dangerous posture reverting back to terrorist tactics involving the use of suicide bombers and IEDs to inflict casualties on ISAF forces."[29]

And then there was some question as to how many of the Taliban had escaped. How decisive was the defeat of the Taliban? Lieutenant-Colonel Lavoie commented on the ability to "cut-off" the enemy. He noted in an insurgency that is very difficult to accomplish. "That's probably one of the weaknesses in the plan overall," he conceded. "There was never really a plan to cut them off, to prevent them from seeping out and escaping." The coalition forces pushed from the north and the southeast, but in the end it came down to tactical aviation to tighten the cordon and prevent enemy from leaking out because there were not enough ground forces to do the job. NATO's failure, or more accurately the failure of European countries, to step up and commit combat troops to the fight resulted in an inability to close the trap.

Lavoie confirmed that there was an overreliance on tactical aviation to prevent the Taliban from escaping to the west. "Although tac[tical] aviation intercepted, killed and destroyed quite a few of them there were still quite a lot who escaped." He added, "We really needed a ground force to be put in there, but it comes down to the fact that we really didn't have the forces to do it."[30]

The other problem the BG CO observed was that of identifying the enemy. "I had a sub-unit screening my left flank 15–20 kilometres away and their job was to contain the seepage," he stated. "They could just report that 30 fighting age 'farmers' were leaving the area, but in accordance with their rules of engagement, because they were unarmed, they couldn't engage them." The frustrated CO questioned, "What could you do to these guys? … You were always certain that they were Taliban, but they're just walking down the highway."[31] As a result, in the words of Lieutenant-Colonel Schreiber, "the enemy [could] just melt away."[32]

Lavoie explained that it is cases such as this where host-nation forces from the ANSF are critical. "They are culturally familiar with their fellow countrymen and always seem to have a sixth sense," he stated. "These guys [ANSF], either through intuition or certainly after talking to suspects, just know that they're not farmers … we [coalition forces] just can't do that." For precisely that reason, Lavoie argued that all operations must be done in conjunction with host-nation forces. "We need the ANSF to act as cut-off groups," he insisted, "so that they can question and identify individuals fleeing a combat area."[33] But the problem was simply a dire shortage of ANSF available to assist.

The enemy seepage was frustrating to the Canadian soldiers, but so was the subsequent exploitation. "We cleared large areas such as Siah Choy and left sub-units there," explained Lieutenant-Colonel Lavoie, "but then Brigade ordered them out and the Taliban flowed in immediately behind the withdrawing troops." He grimaced. "Now we must go and retake them again, compound by compound … the worst part in Siah Choy was that the population started to warm up and support us but once we abandoned them the Taliban returned and killed those who were friendly."[34]

From Lieutenant-Colonel Lavoie's perspective the operation should have continued until the whole campaign was complete. He felt the battle group "should have exploited another 20 kilometres to actually seal off an area to disrupt their [Taliban] lines of communication."[35] He acknowledged that that meant there would have been a lot more fighting at the time, "but we had them on the run and we probably could have kept that pursuit and then actually held the ground we seized and put the Taliban in a position where they would not have been unable to come back into the area." He concluded, "That would have saved us from our current position where we are going back into the same ground we had already cleared … I'm trying to impress upon them [higher headquarters] that we just don't want to disrupt Taliban operations, we actually want to clear and secure the area and prevent the reoccupation [by the Taliban] down the road." He concluded, "In a non-linear battlefield, exploitation is much more important and more complex — it's not about just capturing a piece of ground."[36]

Nonetheless, Lieutenant-Colonel Omer Lavoie and his TF rolled into Phase IV of Operation Medusa after defeating the entrenched Taliban forces in a bitter struggle. In his formal war diary entry Omer Lavoie wrote, "It will take several months to repair the damage done to the local villages in Pashmul and surrounding area but with the Taliban routed from there and my centre of gravity secured once again, I can now begin looking at strengthening the zone around Kandahar City and shifting back to pre-Medusa dispositions."[37] But, Lavoie was not misled by what he and his soldiers accomplished. "Phase IV of Operation Medusa, reconstruction, is the most important, that will actually defeat vice just killing the enemy,"[38] he commented.

But Lavoie was not convinced that the security conditions necessary for reconstruction were entirely met. Despite Lavoie's concern, ISAF declared victory and placed an emphasis on returning the civilian population to the area and creating freedom of action for the GoA and development agencies in order to set the necessary preconditions for the establishment of the Kandahar Advanced Development Zone. As always, higher headquarters focus more on the operational and strategic requirements and tend not to get mired in the tactical battle. As such, as far as they were concerned they had declared victory and it was time to move on with reconstruction.

However, the Taliban was not convinced that they had been defeated. And they were not prepared to surrender the Pashmul area to the Government of Afghanistan or the coalition forces. One Taliban fighter stated, "No Muslim wants the human garbage of foreign soldiers in Afghanistan." He explained, "We were ready to fight, but there was lots of bombs, lots of dust. It was hard to see. So we decided to fight somewhere else."[39] Another Taliban insurgent, named Ashoor, laughed, "You cannot stop us. We've been using these tactics for hundreds of years and they have always worked. ... After an attack fighters can easily stash their weapons among villagers sympathetic to their cause [and] they can then melt in with the local population and move on to another village, where there are more caches of weapons available to them for mounting another attack."[40]

So, despite the declaration of victory there was some confusion about the long-term impact or whether the successful actions by Canadian and coalition forces in Pashmul between 3 and 14 September 2006 actually constituted a victory. Although they had soundly defeated the Taliban's attempt at concentrating forces and holding ground, they had also pushed the Taliban to evolve into a much more dangerous and difficult foe to fight. In essence, Operation Medusa forced the Taliban to adopt asymmetric attacks as their operational methodology. The fight was about to evolve into a much more complex, frustrating, difficult, and dangerous war.

CHAPTER NINE:

The Reality of the Long War

WHILE MAJOR COMBAT OPERATIONS were over on 14 September, the Taliban did not seem to accept their defeat. In fact, it was the period of reconstruction that proved to be deadlier than Operation Medusa itself, as a combination of roadside bombs and suicide bombers, as well as combat and mine strikes, killed another 10 Canadian soldiers in the month following the capture of Objective Rugby. "Kinetically we had great effect," professed Lieutenant-Colonel Peter Williams, "in stark terms, the number of casualties we inflicted on the enemy was significant. We disrupted their leadership to the point where they realized from a conventional point of view they would not be able to take us on and achieve any sort of success." However, he conceded, "we found that they tended to reverse their tactics ... so after Medusa there has been an increase in the number of IEDs and suicide bombers and so on."[1]

In the end, regardless of any long-term assessment of the success of Operation Medusa, it was critical to both the Government of Afghanistan and to the NATO alliance itself. And the two week ordeal was, in the words of Major Marty Lipcsey, the deputy commanding officer of TF 3-06, "quite a battle."[2] The brunt of the combat was born by the soldiers of the 1 RCR Battle Group, TF 3-06. Lieutenant-Colonel Lavoie's assessment that "the soldiers under my command have proven their courage and determination time and time again," was not based on false pride.[3]

But before Phase IV of Operation Medusa was fully underway the reality of the "long war" quickly became apparent to the Canadians and their NATO allies.[4] The struggle took an exponentially more difficult and dangerous turn. The enemy, faced with his lopsided defeat in Panjwayi, learned the lesson that he could not face NATO forces in a traditional, conventional attritional confrontation. The Taliban transitioned, as mentioned by Lieutenant-Colonel Williams, to more asymmetric means utilizing suicide bombers, IEDs, and intimidation of the local populace. "The Taliban reverted to their asymmetric tactics, which had made them far more dangerous," acknowledged Lieutenant-Colonel Schreiber, the MNB operations officer. "They've now re-infiltrated into this area, small groups of highly motivated fighters, tier one Taliban, many of them foreign fighters, Chechens, Tagiks, Arabs and they're now conducting a very effective asymmetric campaign that relies mostly on IEDs and IED ambushes."[5] Intelligence officer Captain Tim Button assessed, "Medusa achieved a 12 month effect. We watched how the Taliban changed the way they did business in a major way." Button emphasized, "We will never again see them mass together to attack. We drove their commanders underground and they were unable to openly exercise their command. But not concentrating force also makes it harder to find them. We reinforced their need to act asymmetrically ... We don't see large opportunities to target them."[6] The Taliban also focused on disrupting reconstruction. The Taliban tactics had become more difficult to counter and made the struggle for the support of the local people increasingly difficult.

Although senior Afghan and NATO officials had declared victory and started to pushed for reconstruction to begin, it was not quite as simple as that. Reconstruction and development were key drivers to winning the support of the people or, in the popular jargon, their "hearts and minds." After all, it was important to demonstrate to the Afghans that there was benefit in supporting the government and coalition efforts — specifically, an increase in their standard of living. Up to that time all that the local nationals had seen was the destruction caused by the fighting. And, despite Brigadier-General Fraser's observation that "there has been battlefield damage largely because of where the Taliban went" and his pledge that "we will go back out there and we will help rebuild that,"[7] the locals saw ISAF as largely responsible for the damage. More importantly, reparations seemed slow in coming.

The delay was not due to a lack of will on the part of ISAF or NATO at large. Senior commanders and politicians pushed hard for reconstruction to begin. However, "it's quite easy to kill people and break things compared to putting them back together," noted Schreiber.[8] The commanding officer of TF 3-06, Lieutenant-Colonel Lavoie lamented, "We are under pressure to get on with reconstruction." He understood it was "important for domestic consumption," however, his problem, as he identified it, was that the "fight isn't won yet." He explained, that the Taliban "was still very strong" and added that the enemy "must be defeated first for lasting reconstruction."[9]

What many unfamiliar with counter-insurgency fail to realize is that security and development are not mutually exclusive activities. Rather, they are mutually supporting. There is no reconstruction and development without security, and no security without reconstruction and development. Each feeds the other. The local population must feel secure and safe from Taliban retribution if they are to assist the government and coalition efforts. Without adequate protection they will remain neutral and aloof at best, or at worst, passively or actively support the insurgent efforts.[10] Haji Gailani questioned, "You have planes. You can hear the Taliban on your radios. And still you cannot force them out of here. How can we?"[11] As one authoritative report concluded, "Security is the most basic precondition for civilian support of the government ... the motivation that provides the only real long lasting effect is the elemental consideration of survival."[12]

Without the support of the people, it becomes difficult, if not impossible, to gain intelligence on enemy activity and intentions. A lot of effort has to be put into force protection, which detracts from reconstruction and development since there are finite resources in theatre. More importantly, it becomes extremely difficult to determine who is actually the enemy. "We're trying to win the hearts and minds of the people," insisted Lavoie, "yet, we have to defend against the asymmetric threat."[13] One of his subordinates was blunter: "We still think everyone approaching us wants to kill us," explained Captain Ryan Carey. "We have no choice but to plan for a fight right till we leave."[14]

For the soldiers in the field, like those before them who have struggled with counter-insurgency throughout history, it was the asymmetric nature of the conflict that created both frustrations as well as tangible delays in advancing the reconstruction and development agenda. Lavoie shrugged his shoulders as he admitted there was a full range of problems he and his troops faced. "The greatest source of frustration is intelligence," he conceded. "There is frustration working in an environment where it is so difficult to identify friend from foe." He explained, "Within Patrol Base Wilson (PBW) we know there are Taliban operatives ... When senior ANA or ANP officers in the headquarters are sending the Taliban information on our plans it's difficult to operate." Moreover, he added, "in the field a farmer drops his shovel and picks up an AK-47 and transitions from a non-combatant to a combatant seamlessly."[15]

One young officer reinforced, "You don't know who your enemy is. One minute they will be walking down the street and have a woman and children surrounding them and the next the woman and children will disappear and he [the enemy] will be firing at you."[16] A British non-commissioned officer (NCO) described:

> It was a real 360 degree battlefield out there. You never know where it is going to come from. The Taliban are quite good at getting behind you. Snap ambushes are what they are good at. We are getting dicked [informed on] all the time. They use a cordless phone with a 30 km range on it. As soon as we left somewhere and went anywhere, they knew about it. Their network was awesome and it aided them in laying ambushes and IEDs.
>
> They attack you when you are least expecting it. We made two mistakes and they punished us for that.[17]

But the pressures, strains, and realities of the soldier fighting the battle and those of their superiors are not the same. In fact, they are not even compatible and the divergence between immediate interests and requirements grows wider as one rises up the hierarchal chain of command. To Lavoie and his men survival is a key, if not the primary, concern. They fought the daily running battle with the Taliban and knew, regardless of the press reports and what their superiors were saying, that the Taliban was still very much active and deadly in their area of operations.

However, Lavoie faced a cascading flow of scepticism and concern, starting from political masters in a number of NATO countries, including his own, down through their national, as well as NATO, command chains. All were clamouring for results. It was not enough to declare victory in the press — NATO had to actually show it. Anxious to demonstrate that progress was being made to placate demanding national governments and politicians, the pressure on field commanders was enormous.

Lavoie constantly felt the pressure. "It's hard to convince headquarters of the reality on the ground," bemoaned Lavoie. "They've never been forward — they have not visited the troops forward, yet they don't believe I can't start phase IV reconstruction even though I've lost seven guys on this road [Route Summit]."[18] Route Summit was a new road that he was building between Highway 1 and Ma'Sūm Ghar in Pashmul, in order to increase security and provide a better road network to assist economic development in the area. The road project was a direct result of Operation Medusa.[19] The BG had lost some men on the existing road in Pashmul because it was narrow and cut through close country, which was ideal for ambushes and IED placement. The governor had not come through with the promised ANA or ANP support to monitor the existing road so Lavoie decided to find an alternate route. He checked with brigade headquarters and no one said no, so he began to cut a great swath through the local cannabis fields.[20]

"I never thought I would be doing this," shrugged Lavoie. "We're supposed to be doing Phase IV resettlement and reconstruction and the ANA are supposed to do security but they haven't shown up." Lavoie pointed out, "Building the road is the only way to do it." He explained it was short-term security for the region and his forward operating base (FOB) at Ma'Sūm Ghar, and long-term development and security for Pashmul as it provided access on a defendable high-speed road.[21]

But the project also had a negative side. With very few ANSF to assist with the static defence and security of the project, Lavoie was forced to use his battle group, already anaemic due to the casualties sustained during Operation Medusa, which had not yet been replaced, and the commencement of the home leave travel allowance (HLTA) rotation system, which sent complete sections out of theatre at a time.[22] Low on manpower and with virtually no assistance from the ANSF, Task Force 3-06 was forced to take up static locations at various FOBs and strong points to defend the road construction.[23] Therefore, they surrendered the initiative and the ability to dominate the ground and became static targets tied to infrastructure.

To aggravate the situation even more, Lavoie noted that higher head-quarters consistently tried to assign additional tasks, despite Lavoie's forces being stretched thin to provide security over the road construc-tion and other FOBs within his AOR, all a direct result of a failure of host nation forces being made available to undertake static security tasks.[24] "NATO headquarters," Lavoie lamented, "often are unrealistic in their taskings — too often they have too great an appetite ... I've had to say no on a number of occasions."[25] Lavoie sadly pointed out, "I've been for-ward on 15 of the 17 KIA [killed in action] to see the bodies being put into the body bags ... That's a lot different than a casket being loaded on an airplane." With frustration Lavoie insisted that "Higher HQ needs to see that." He explained that that he was having difficulty convincing his seniors of the reality on the ground. "They've never been forward, the commander has not visited the troops forward, he hasn't seen the road ... I lost seven guys out here and he's never come," lamented the CO, "[yet he] doesn't believe we can't start Phase IV reconstruction."[26]

And so, with the kinetic phase of Operation Medusa behind them, the soldiers of the 1 RCR BG began transitioning into the "long war." Trying to both support reconstruction and development, as well as secure the wider area and fight the Taliban, TF 3-06 soon found them-selves tied down in a static posture, which provided the enemy with the initiative. Embedded reporter Les Perreaux observed, "In those 19 days, soldiers attacked mercilessly to drive out Taliban forces and [then] watched helplessly as the Taliban drifted back in."[27] Not surprisingly, the Taliban seized on the opportunity and attempted to gain their own retri-bution for their costly defeat in September.

The daily routine soon turned into one of tedium punctuated by moments of terror. Soldiers endured the relentless heat and tolerated the irritating and constant dust churned up by any movement whether vehicle, human, or wind. The fine talcum-powder-like sand covered everything and it was impossible to keep anything clean. To add to the misery, the unremitting sand fleas and flies tortured the soldiers without pause.

Nonetheless, TF 3-06, which had an area of operations spanning approximately 60,000 square kilometres, found itself protecting Route Summit, which cut a 100 metre wide swath straight through the marijuana fields and vineyards. Its wide berth and straight trajectory provided easy observation, control, and security. More importantly, this easily accessible road, which would eventually be paved, would furnish local farmers with an excellent route that would allow produce and trade to transit quickly from the fertile Arghandab River valley to Highway 1, the major artery leading to Kandahar City and elsewhere.

The brunt of the defence of the road fell to Charles Coy Gp. They soon found themselves in a constant battle of wits with the enemy. The Taliban harassed the thinly stretched troops persistently. During the night they would stealthily plant IEDs and mines in the sandy furrow that represented the road. In addition, the Taliban deployed small teams that would attempt to surprise and ambush the Canadian troops. They had already immobilized two bulldozers and several other vehicles through IED and mine strikes.

The terrain once again assisted the insurgents. The tall-marijuana fields and vineyards, interspersed with mud walls and sun baked mud huts that had the consistency of fortified strongholds, obscured visibility and allowed the Taliban concealed and protected manoeuvre space. Armed with the initiative and forgiving terrain, the Taliban kept up a constant pressure, hitting particularly hard on 14 October 2006, in an example of their increasing sophistication.

The day started like so many others. Lieutenant-Colonel Lavoie rolled down the sandy strip that revealed the beginnings of the new road with his four vehicle convoy to coordinate with his sub-units and verify defences and progress being made. He quickly came across C/S 33A. Their LAV III, which was located half way between the 7 and 9 Platoons positions, had backed over an IED and the vehicle had become a mobility kill. Luckily, no one was injured. Unfortunately, the TF had just lost another precious vehicle that would be hard to replace.

The IED had been placed in the middle of the unfinished road, about 400 metres from 7 Platoon's defensive position, which was co-located with a small ANA detachment. Everyone was mystified as to how that had transpired. How had the "ghosts of Panjwayi" planted it without being seen? But an IED strike was not an uncommon occurrence and efforts soon turned to recovering the vehicle back to Patrol Base Wilson.

As the morning wore on, members of 7 Platoon continued with their surveillance duty in the growing heat. Those not on duty within the LAV III or sentry positions sheltered themselves under a tarp behind the protection of a low wall that was situated between two buildings that had been partially destroyed during Operation Medusa. On the opposite side of the wall ran a canal in which an ANA detachment had taken residence. The ANA manned several OPs that were constructed to control the old road and the terrain to the west.

The members of the platoon had been in the field in this threat environment for 23 days straight. They slept, ate, and tried to relax in the filth that surrounded them. They slept on Therm-a-Rest mattresses on the ground with their body armour at their side. Water was in short supply, and facilities were lacking — washing clothes was unheard of and even personal hygiene was limited. The incessant dust covered everything and made maintenance of weapons and vehicles a constant concern. Conditions were primitive to say the least.

At approximately 1100 hours, a radio message arrived stating that a group of three Taliban had been seen to the west of 7 Platoon's position. Warrant Officer Ray McFarlane, the Platoon warrant/second-in-command (2IC), and Sergeant Donovan Crawford quickly coordinated with the ANA detachment. After patiently trying to convey the message to the ANA leader, who understood some English, and with a large degree of innovative sign language, the message was passed and the ANA mobilized. With members of 7 Platoon close by, with their 60mm mortar ready to engage in the fight, the ANA sent a small patrol out several hundred metres from the position to investigate the sighting.

A short time later excited voices could be heard close by, followed by the "whoosshh" and explosion of an RPG 7 rocket and the crack of some small-arms fire. Within minutes the ANA soldiers returned with great big smiles gesturing with a wave of the hand and a simple "Taliban gone." McFarlane was unable to ascertain whether the Taliban had been killed or simply scattered. Each question elicited the same grunts and nodding of heads from the ANA patrol. Nonetheless, the threat seemed to have dissipated for the moment.

Meanwhile, several kilometres down the road to the south, 9 Platoon (C/S 33) manned their position. It was given the designation "Strong Point Centre," aptly named since it was the middle position within the Battle Group's defensive network that followed the path of the new road from PBW on Highway 1 to the imposing Ma'Sūm Ghar mountain feature where "A" Company, which had been seconded from the 2 PPCLI, was constructing the new FOB Zettelmeyer, named after the engineer vehicle that was struck on 3 September. Strong Point Centre was a formidable position based around an imposing mud structure built on a small outcropping that dominated the road and the surrounding area.

The platoon used the natural lay of the land to anchor their defence. Two LAV IIIs flanked the position and covered the western approach and the road. To their front lay a 100 metre swath of sand and beyond that marijuana fields, vineyards, and an array of mud compounds and grape-drying huts. Visibility was limited. Sheltered behind the large mud building that was the centre point of the defensive position and protected by a natural wall to its other side, another LAV III aimed its deadly 25mm cannon to the north, covering the road approach. Finally, dug into the raised island that was Strong Point Centre were two machine-gun pits. One faced south to control the road while the other faced east to cover the close terrain, mainly vineyards, which bordered right up to the defensive position. The platoon had augmented the natural fortress with a series of sandbagged walls.

Much like 7 Platoon, the soldiers of 9 Platoon rotated between sentry duty in the LAVs or in the machine gun posts and catching up on sleep or a meal. Manpower was especially tight since the section in the IED strike in the morning were back at PBW getting medically checked out

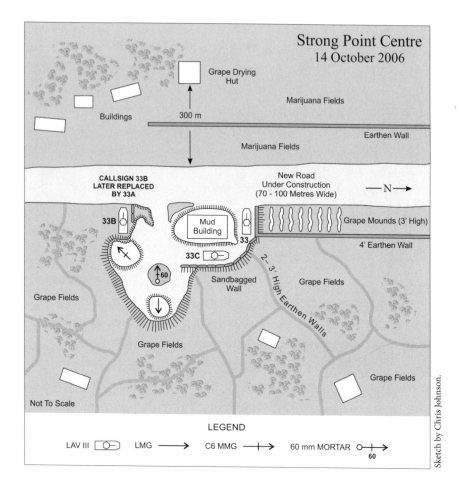

Strong Point Centre
14 October 2006

Not To Scale

LEGEND

LAV III   LMG ⟶   C6 MMG ⊢→   60 mm MORTAR ⊶⊢→

Sketch by Chris Johnson.

for any injuries sustained during the blast. The incidents of the morning seemed to harbour no sinister omen and were largely forgotten. After all, those types of events were virtually everyday occurrences.

Back at 7 Platoon, at approximately 1430 hours, the gunner in the turret of the LAV covering south along the road and the vast fields to the east summoned Warrant Officer McFarlane. Out in the vineyards, approximately 200–300 metres away, six men, ostensibly "farmers," as they carried no weapons, calmly walked south through the fields in single file towards a large grape-drying hut located approximately 400 metres from 7 Platoon's position. Rules of Engagement (ROEs) forbid firing on unarmed civilians regardless of how suspicious they appeared. The Taliban were aware of that and utilized their ability to blend in with the normal farmers to their advantage. Identifying friend from foe is one of the greatest challenges in that environment. The TF soldiers observed fighting-age males in the fields on many occasions, but whether they were legitimate farmers or Taliban posing as such was difficult to ascertain. With cached weapons throughout the area, the enemy could transform from one to the other and back again very quickly. Determining who was the enemy, as well as being able to physically dominate the ground and sweep it for weapons, was almost impossible due to the shortage of personnel.

Lacking the manpower to send a patrol to investigate, McFarlane attempted to convince the ANA to follow-up; however, the ANA claimed they too lacked the troops to wander out into the fields to scrutinize the suspicious party. Quite simply, without direct Canadian participation they would not venture out. McFarlane was forced to try and keep surveillance on the individuals as long as possible since he was unable to take any other action. Not surprisingly, the "farmers" quickly melted away into the maze of walls, buildings, and vegetation.

At approximately 1450 hours, some visitors (i.e., members of the PRT and some local Afghan officials) started to congregate at the front of Strong Point Centre. They were awaiting the CO's convoy for a ride back to PBW. Lieutenant Ray Corby, the 9 Platoon commander, had taken over the platoon three weeks prior when the casualties incurred in the early days of Operation Medusa triggered a reshuffling of personnel. While waiting for the vehicles to arrive, Corby made an effort to speak to the visiting district chief but was brushed off. Corby then turned his attention to the Civil Military Cooperation (CIMIC) detachment commander, Chief Warrant Officer Fred Gratton. However, he was interrupted three times in a span of less than 10 minutes by the district chief, who persistently asked when his ride would be arriving. During that same period the district chief received two phone calls on his cellphone and placed another call himself. He seemed desperately eager to leave.

The CO arrived at Strong Point Centre at approximately 1455 hours and dismounted to briefly discuss details of the earlier IED incident with Lieutenant Corby while the visiting personnel at the location loaded onto the vehicles that made up the CO's tactical HQ (or 9er Tac). Just as the vehicles were in the midst of loading, a threat warning came over the air, "a Canadian position was in imminent threat of attack." The grid given was uncomfortably close to their current position. The soldiers had learned to dread the threat warnings — they were usually accurate. Inside Strong Point Centre the warning was verbally relayed to Corby. As he formulated his next course of action, the initiative was wrested away from him. Less than a minute passed from the time he was given the notice to all hell breaking loose.

The initial barrage of enemy fire caught the soldiers of "C" Coy by surprise. The attack commenced with multiple RPGs being fired at the position. A minimum of three RPGs were fired in close succession, targeting C/S 33B, which was manning the southwest perimeter of the position, an empty trench on the western flank of the strongpoint, and the OP on the southeast of the defensive position that contained a C-6 GPMG. A high volume of small-arms fire also hit the position; some rounds impacted short and kicked up the dust on the new road while others cracked over the heads of the "C" Coy troops.

Lieutenant Corby was in the midst of discussing the platoon's course of action with Sergeant Jamie Walsh. As the RPG rockets and small-arms fire rained in, reaction was immediate. Corby and Walsh dove for cover behind a small berm located behind C/S 33C, which was the LAV in the centre of the position. From that vantage point, looking towards the southwest, they could see smoke coming from the treeline and marijuana fields, as well as rounds splashing across the sand of the new road towards them. Visibility was quickly obscured as the dust was kicked up by the fire. Nevertheless, it seemed the concentration of the enemy attack was coming from the west. The insurgents had the bright sun at their backs to mask their movement and blind the defenders.

The Canadians on sentry duty responded with alacrity. The 25mm cannons on the LAVs, aided by their thermal sights, which could see through the dust, thundered in reply, supported by light-machine guns and GPMGs, while the others quickly manned their fighting positions. When the storm struck, Private Jesse Larochelle was in the south-most machine-gun pit. The enemy attack washed over him like a rogue wave. His position erupted in explosions, as bullets and shrapnel hissed through the air around him. Larochelle thought he was hallucinating as he saw seemingly mini-explosions go off above his outpost. At the time he didn't realize that the enemy was using RPG munitions that emitted mini cluster rounds from its 75mm warhead, which exploded, spraying deadly shrapnel much like an air-burst round. Despite the weight of fire, Larochelle continued to fire at his invisible antagonists who were cloaked by the treeline.

Close by, the CO's tactical HQ had just started to roll when a RPG rocket swished to the rear and exploded in a ball of flame approximately 80 metres behind the convoy, where mere minutes prior the CO, platoon commander, and others had been standing. The three LAVs and the RG-31 Nyala armoured vehicle, which made up the tactical HQ, quickly swung around and immediately began to engage the enemy, adding an enormous amount of fire into the fields and buildings to the west where the enemy assault was originating.

Unfortunately, the retaliation was a bit too late. As the "pum-pum-pum" of the 25mm cannons echoed across the battlefield, the first SITREP cut through the noise and hit everyone as if they had been struck through the heart with a spike — "two VSA [vital signs absent], three wounded." Stark reality once again set in. As Operation Medusa had shown, the Taliban are little match for the Western forces in either equipment or firepower. They rely on surprise, either through IEDs, mines, or ambushes. And they depend on achieving success in the first 30 seconds of the engagement before they become engulfed in return fire. Once again they got lucky.

The crew and section of C/S 33B were resting when the attack commenced. Private Jesse Kezar was in the driver's hatch and Corporal Jeremy Penney was in the gunner's seat when the initial barrage of fire hit. Penney attempted to fire the 25mm gun but the cannon jammed. Corporal Darryl Jones was in the process of moving into the turret from the rear of the LAV when the RPG round struck around the vehicle's laser warning tower. The resulting explosion showered the area with shrapnel. Lethal shards of metal and blast washed down through the rear-air-sentry hatch and over the back deck, killing one soldier who had been seated on the left bench and wounding another who was seated on the right bench. The same round also killed the section commander and wounded two others who were at the back of the LAV.

At exactly the same time, 1500 hours, 7 Platoon was also hit. PKM machine-gun fire and RPGs engulfed the surprised troops. Bullets stitched their way along the wall that soldiers had rested against earlier, kicking up dirt and forcing all to find cover. The fire emanated from the grape-drying hut where the six "farmers" were seen heading earlier. The platoon replied in rapid succession bringing all of its firepower, as well as that of the neighbouring ANA, to bear. During the contact as many as 20–30 enemy were sighted in that area alone. Notwithstanding the enemy's strength, the situation was brought under control.

Back at 9 Platoon, Sergeant Walsh organized his section to better engage the enemy in their location. He placed Corporal Nick Damchuk, and Privates Jay Royer and Garret Achneepineskum behind a small berm directly behind his LAV C/S 33C, where they laid down suppressing fire to the area west of the stronghold. Walsh then deployed Corporal Chris Saumure and Private Ed Runyon-Lloyd at the front of the LAV to observe for enemy activity to the east of the position. Corporal Mike Lisk was in the turret of C/S 33C and he was soon joined by Master-Corporal Rob Murphy who used the small escape hatch on the side of the LAV to crawl up into the turret. Due to the lack of enemy activity in their primary arcs to the northeast of the position, Murphy traversed the turret over the back deck of the LAV so that the cannon could be fired to the southwest. He then used the height of the pintle-mounted machine gun to fire over the high feature to their front to add extra firepower to the fight. All the while, Corporal Jeff Morin was redistributing ammunition to the section as the scale of the combat quickly depleted the immediate supply.

Simultaneously, Lieutenant Corby quickly moved to his HQ LAV, sited on the north side of the position, to ensure a contact report had been sent out. As he neared his vehicle he could see they were busy engaging a large number of enemy directly to the west. Corporal Morgan Gonci had been in the driver's hatch prior to the attack. As the first few rockets exploded nearby he could feel the LAV shake. Corporal James White, observing from the gunner's seat, also felt C/S 33 reel as an RPG rocket hit the front, right side of the LAV, ripping off some of its up-armour plating. With the onset of the attack Sergeant Craig Dinsmore crawled up through the rear of the vehicle into the crew commander's seat and

Corporal Gonci immediately began to provide target indication from the driver's hatch. At the same time, Corporals Shane Robertson and Joey Paolini jumped into the back of LAV and raised the ramp. As Corby arrived he banged repeatedly on the back door until it was opened. He then instructed Robertson and Paolini to provide security to the north of C/S 33 to ensure the enemy did not outflank their position.

Corby took a headset and sent a supplementary contact report on the company net. He also requested a fire mission, sending his exact location, the distance to the enemy, and the bearing of 4,800 mils. Fortuitously, Major Greg Ivey, G29 the CO's affiliated battery commander who travelled in the 9er Tac convoy, was already in the process of calling in artillery support. Within 10 minutes of the start of the engagement, 155mm rounds exploded with an earth shaking "krummpp" 400 metres away from Strong Point Centre, dangerously close. Word was passed over the net that "AH" (Apache attack helicopters) were on their way.

Satisfied that the call for fire was taken care of, Corby tried to raise his sections on the radio to get a more accurate read on the battle. He began with the OP with the GPMG as it had the highest vantage point. He became concerned when he received no reply. His second call went to C/S 33B to the south of the position. Corby received a SITREP from Corporal Jones, who was in the turret of the 2 Section LAV. Jones informed the platoon commander that they had two casualties, vital signs absent. He also requested a medic to look after the other three wounded soldiers. Corby questioned Jones on the extent of the other injuries and determined that they were not critical.

Luckily there was an advanced qualified soldier to administer first aid. However, he, Master-Corporal Jeremy Leblanc, was in dire need of additional medical supplies. Corby decided not to risk his only medic by sending her across exposed terrain, in light of the heavy volume of enemy fire. Instead, Corby grabbed the medical bag and made his way to 2 Section's location himself.

Meanwhile Paolini and Robertson, on the outside of the HQ vehicle, were busy engaging the enemy. Between the two soldiers they saw two separate groups, five individuals in total, with small arms and RPGs engaging their position.

Out on the road, the CO's convoy continued to pour fire into the buildings, wood line, and marijuana fields. At about that time, Corby moved back to C/S 33C, which occupied the centre of the platoon position. He looked across at C/S 33B and could see that the turret was still firing. He quickly informed Sergeant Walsh of his plan to run the medical bag first to the OP and then to C/S 33B's location. Damchuk and Achneepineskum laid down a wall of suppressive fire as Corby made his mad dash.

To get to 2 Section's LAV he first had to pass by the southernmost OP. Corby did not expect to find anyone alive. As he arrived at the bowl in the centre of the strongpoint position, which was also the casualty collection point, Corby was able to get eyes on the OP. At first glance it had appeared that the OP had been struck hard. He could not see anyone and the tarp that had been hung above the outpost to provide shade had been torn away by the fire and it hung in tattered rags. Close by he could see the empty casings of four M72 launchers.

Corby called out twice to the OP. He finally got a response. Private Larochelle poked his head up with his C-6 and confirmed he was "okay" and "by himself." The platoon commander directed Larochelle to provide covering fire so he could enter the OP. Larochelle pointed out where he had been engaging the enemy with his C-9 LMG, the C-6 GPMG, and the M72s. The firefight had been so brisk that Larochelle was down to his last half belt of 7.62mm GPMG ammunition. He had weathered the storm and continued to fire at any movement or weapon signature he could see. He also maintained his discipline and continued to observe his arcs of fire in order to ensure that no enemy was approaching from the east, even though he was taking heavy fire from the west.

Corby was humbled by the young soldier's valiant efforts.[28] However, he had no time to reflect on Larochelle's courage — there was work to be done. Corby now instructed Larochelle to lay down more fire so he could make his final way to 2 Section's (C/S 33B) LAV. Corby promised that when he returned he would bring additional ammo.

After the first deadly RPG strike, Corporal Jones had remedied the gun malfunction and started to return fire. A second RPG round hit C/S 33B, setting off the automatic fire extinguishing system in the LAV. When

Corby arrived he quickly recognized that they had, in fact, suffered two killed. Master-Corporal Leblanc, who himself was wounded, had bandaged up the casualties, while the rest of the section were on the line, busy returning fire from a sandbagged wall they had constructed adjacent to the LAV position. Once patched up, Corporals Chris Dowhan and Chris Meace joined their section on the firing line.

By that time the "C" Coy soldiers were about 15–20 minutes into the fight. Corby now sent another SITREP to his company HQ. He learned that the company second-in-command was on the scene with numerous other LAVs to lend a hand. Corby recommended that they form a firing line north of his position and orient themselves to the southwest so that they could assist in suppressing the enemy's heavy fire into Strong Point Centre.

As the battle dispositions were discussed, Jones reported a second stoppage of the cannon. Master-Corporal Leblanc, despite his wounds, switched places with Jones in an attempt to rectify the stoppage. However, since he was becoming faint and weak from loss of blood, Leblanc was pulled from the turret and Jones returned to do what he could.

Lieutenant Corby was happy to learn that 1 Section, who had hit the IED in the morning, were on their way back out with a replacement LAV, which had just arrived in theatre, fresh off the assembly line from London, Ontario. However, his morale took a hit when he heard that the Bison ambulance that accompanied it was now disabled due to a mechanical breakdown. Corby decided to use the battle damaged C/S 33B to evacuate the dead and wounded to PBW. That would get his men back to PBW for medical attention quickly and C/S 33A could provide the necessary reinforcements and added firepower

By then the Taliban were largely suppressed. The weight of fire and dreaded artillery, which impeded insurgent movement, swung the battle to the advantage of the TF 3-06 soldiers. But that was no surprise to the Taliban. They were very aware of coalition tactics, techniques, and procedures (TTPs) and knew exactly how long it would take coalition resources to be fed into the battle. To further complicate the response, the Taliban often coordinated attacks to buy themselves more time. Today, they hit simultaneously at five different locations throughout the AO.

With the enemy suppressed and the dead and wounded evacuated, Corby's thoughts turned to securing the position for the night. His position remained on "100 percent stand-to." To ensure he could hold the position, reinforcements and a resupply of ammunition was brought into the strong point. In addition, F-18 and F-16 fighter aircraft remained on station the entire night, providing observation and fire when required. At one point an air strike lit up the darkness with a bright orange wall of flame — a beautiful sight in a rather macabre sort of way. To the soldiers holding the road, the sound of fighter aircraft streaking overhead was reassuring.

At 0700 hours, 4 Platoon arrived to relieve the exhausted 9 Platoon. The relief in place went smoothly. 4 Platoon already had a section in place, which had been brought in during the night as reinforcements, and the entire platoon had already done a stint of duty at Strong Point Centre several weeks earlier. For 9 Platoon it was a bittersweet moment; they had weathered the storm well and shown resilience and courage but tragically, they lost another two of their comrades.

The attack on 14 October 2006 was one of the larger attacks. But the war of the flea continued with the Taliban continuing its incessant attacks on the Canadians who were stuck guarding infrastructure. By the end of November, approximately two months after the end of Operation Medusa, Lieutenant-Colonel Don Bolduc, CO of the 1st Bn, 3 SFG (Desert Eagles) estimated the strength of Taliban back in the Pashmul area at 800.[29] As a result, another operation was required to try and clear out the insurgents to allow for reconstruction and development.

Regional Headquarters (South) (RC [S]), which became the formal title of the formation headquarters, replacing the MNB HQ title once NATO took full responsibility for Afghanistan in October 2006, set about preparing for another large operation. It assessed that a high level of insurgent activity continued to emanate from the Zhari/Panjwayi Districts. The formation-level staff officers claimed that although the local population was seeking an end to the violence, there still existed "hard-core" Taliban, assessed as "mostly foreign to the area," who still viewed the areas as a key battleground. As such, ISAF directed planners to create the conditions to force the enemy out of the area to allow the local population to take over responsibility for the first line of security, reinforced by a smaller but enduring presence of ISAF and ANA troops. ISAF deemed this as a pre-condition for further development of the Kandahar ADZ.

The RC(S) assessment underlined what Lavoie had been trying to convince his superiors of for a long time. The formation intelligence officers noted that the insurgents continued to conduct reinforcing and resupply operations with relative ease into the Zhari/Panjwayi Districts as a result of their rat lines coming out of the nearby Registan Desert and other lines of communication to the west. The intelligence analysts concluded that the influx of weapons, particularly mortars, enabled the enemy to conduct frequent attacks against PBW and the other FOBs in the area. They further noted that the Taliban had established a very effective early warning network in the area and were capable of conducting coordinated ambushes on extremely short notice. Moreover, the insurgents could also count on drawing additional fighters from Uruzgan, Helmand, and other areas of Kandahar, as well as Pakistan, to maintain relatively large force levels.

ISAF decided to build on the effects from Operation Medusa to establish an enduring stable environment within the Zhari/Panjwayi Districts to enable the development of the Kandahar ADZ. A senior NATO commander stated that the operation is a "show of unity and strength and a demonstration by ISAF of its ability to combat and defeat the Taliban."[30] ISAF ordered RC(S) to dislocate the "hard-core" (Tier 1) Taliban by separating them from the "local TB" (Tier 2) and the local population on which they depend. This operation was predicated on engagement of local tribal elders to convince them to accept their role in the development of security. Manoeuvre elements would support the initiative by interdicting, disrupting, and destroying Taliban command-and-control nodes and fighters.[31]

Operation Baaz Tsuka was born. Major-General Ton Van Loon, the Dutch ISAF commander, affirmed, "The aim of Baaz Tsuka is twofold, to destroy the Taliban's ability to mount a fresh offensive in the spring, and to encourage Afghan forces to take more control of security in the region." He revealed, "For me, success is when the elders can actually take responsibility for their own security when we can deploy police into the area as much as possible, when we can make sure the Taliban cannot use the window to build up for a spring offensive."[32]

Brigadier-General Tim Grant, the new commander of RC (S) who replaced David Fraser when he rotated out of theatre, insisted, "I'm still hopeful the plan laid out by General Van Loon will allow us to achieve the aim of dislocating the Taliban and have the village elders take more responsibility for influence and security with a minimum of fighting." Grant said the goal was to separate the hard-line Taliban from those who were fighting mainly for the money.[33]

The colourful and gregarious Canadian chief of the Defence Staff, General Rick Hillier, was predictably more direct. He put the operation in more understandable language, stressing that the principle aim of the operation was to kill Taliban commanders and suicide-bomb makers. "One of the parts of this kind of operation," he explained, "is in particular to neutralize or take out the leaders who plan, prepare, facilitate; who get the money and get the vehicles for people" to conduct suicide bombings.[34]

The 1 RCR BG was once again a key component of the operation. "Having sat on Route Summit for the better part of two months now they're anxious to do something," opined Brigadier-General Grant. He ordered the 1 RCR BG to disrupt insurgent activity in order to set the conditions for the Kandahar City ADZ. The BG, in concert with U.S. and ANA forces, assaulted from east to west to secure villages in the Panjwayi Valley. Once the enemy was forced out of the valley the emphasis transitioned to humanitarian operations. Lieutenant-Colonel Lavoie clearly stated, "We're going to go in as soft as possible but as hard as necessary if they want to make it difficult on us." His hope was to conduct the operation "less kinetic than we did in Medusa."[35]

By 20 December, pronouncements emanating from RC(S) headquarters were positive. They assessed that Phases 1 and 2 of Operation Baaz Tsuka had significantly disrupted local insurgent command and control within the Zhari/Panjwayi region. Moreover, they received reports that insurgents were unsure of how to respond to the new offensive and that the will of the local fighters had started to wane. Intelligent analysts further assessed that insurgents were fleeing westward out of the AO.[36]

The operation once again seemed to provide the chimera of security in the area. It also provided the Government of Afghanistan and ISAF the opportunity to develop a series of fortified checkpoints, each manned by six to eight ANSF personnel about five to seven kilometres apart along the main routes, as part of the long-term security program. But the long war continued. There was no peace. This, however, was nothing new. "There is no single piece of land in this country which has not been occupied by a Soviet soldier," observed Sergei Akhromeev, the Soviet deputy minister of defence, in November 1986. "Nevertheless, the majority of the territory remains in the hands of the rebels ... There is no single military problem that has arisen and that has not been solved, and yet there is still no result ... The whole problem is in the fact that military results are not followed up by political."[37]

The failure of reconstruction and development efforts to make significant inroads was as much a function of an inability to provide the necessary overarching security infrastructure as it was a failure of the Afghan government and the coalition to ensure good governance. "The lack of Afghan government presence and services, its inability to provide adequate security or improve the life of the average citizen with sufficient aid and revenues, [as well as] corruption and ethnic differences creates a vacuum threat forces can exploit," counselled strategic analyst Anthony Cordesman. "Rampant corruption, absence of rule of law, and failure of Government to provide equitable social services are rapidly undermining Afghan popular support for democratic governance model and possibly foreign military presence."[38]

Quite simply, success in the long war depends on the ability of the government to be credible. But, as the International Crisis Group reported, "Today, people are pulling back from a government that is failing them, if not preying on them." A poll taken on 7 December 2006, demonstrated that Afghan "public optimism has declined sharply across Afghanistan." Quite simply, public perception was that security was worsening and there was rising concerns about a resurgent Taliban, and decreasing faith in the government's effectiveness.[39] Two weeks later another poll revealed that only 62 percent of Afghans believed that things were moving in the right direction in Afghanistan. Significantly, that was a dramatic 21 percent drop from the previous year.[40]

So who is winning the long war? "It's not a linear battlefield and it's much harder to measure progress," stated Lavoie. "The enemy has all the assets of an insurgent. One minute he has a hoe in his hand, the next minute it's an AK-47."[41] Ominously, the difficulty in measuring real success prompted some backward thinking. "We were asked to keep track of body counts of Taliban by higher HQ," revealed Lieutenant-Colonel Schreiber, the operations officer at the RC(S) HQ. "We replied that this was meaningless — often inaccurate and it didn't matter anyways as it was not a measure of success. We were told to do it anyways because they needed something quantifiable to tell their higher."[42]

And so the long war dragged on. "The Taliban is learning from their experience [in conflicts with ISAF] in the same way we are and we see increasing use of heavier weapons on their part," stated Brigadier-General Joseph Votel, deputy commander of operations for ISAF's Regional Command East.[43] Another veteran commander conceded, "This is a thinking enemy and we ignore that at our own peril."[44]

"It's difficult, absolutely," confessed Major Todd Scharlach. "They [Taliban] are a smart enemy, they know what they have to do and they're trying everything they can to hurt us."[45] Brigadier-General Fraser agreed. "The enemy is adaptive and intelligent," he readily acknowledged.[46] So, not surprisingly, the Taliban adjusted their methodology to maximize their tactical and strategic effect. For example, in 2005, there had been only 17 suicide attacks. "While there were just two suicide bombings in 2002, there is now one every five days," reported Elizabeth Rubin on 29 October 2006.[47] By the end of November, several months after Operation Medusa, there were a total of 106 suicide attacks.[48] In December 2006, the Center for Strategic and International Studies in Washington, D.C., assessed, "The reconstituted enemy is more lethal and shows increased capacity for effective asymmetric warfare, including effective information operations."[49]

Brigadier-General David Fraser, the brigade commander who was responsible for Operation Medusa, captured the frustration of the long war. "The battle was hard, but the reconstruction was harder."[50] Nonetheless he insisted, "We're getting this right. We just have to persevere and stick it out."[51] Fraser warned, however, that "the campaign to help build a nation will not be won this summer or next summer. It will take time ... How much time? As long as it takes."[52] Fraser emphasized, "Counter-insurgency is a marathon — this is really hard stuff."[53]

But to the soldiers the long war that played out after Operation Medusa boiled down to one simple realization: "You roll the dice with your life every time you go outside the wire," stated one Canadian soldier without emotion.[54] And there was little solace to be found in the assessment of Harvard scholar Michael Ignatieff, who announced that "the side that has the greatest willingness to take and inflict casualties in real war is the side that is most likely to prevail."[55] And so the long war continues.

Preparatory bombardment. Objective Rugby is pounded by artillery and close air support, 2 September 2006.

1 RCR BG LAV IIIs on Ma'Sūm Ghar. Evidence of the construction of the location as a more permanent FOB is apparent in the background.

Courtesy 1 RCR BG.

The killing grounds of Bayenzi. The shattered remnants of the white schoolhouse are still clearly visible.

Courtesy "B" Coy, 1 RCR BG.

Elements of 23 Field Engineer Squadron use a dozer to clear a breach on "Cracked Roof" to allow "B" Coy LAV IIIs to advance to support the next tactical bound.

"Fix and Load." Members of "B" Coy Gp prepare to take the next objective.

Members of 3 Section, 4 Platoon "storm the breach," 10 September 2006.

The "ground pounders'" timeless task — "closing with and destroying the enemy."

"The Fog of War." "B" Coy soldiers follow up a preparatory bombardment to clear yet another compound.

Left: An enemy compound burns as members of TF 3-06 prepare to push through to the next objective.

Below: Brigadier-General David Fraser watches operations with Lieutenant-Colonel Steve Williams, commander of TF Grizzly (left), and Lieutenant-Colonel Omer Lavoie, commander TF 3-06 on his right.

Right: A Taliban-fortified entrenchment in Panjwayi.

Below: The map used by RC(S) headquarters to explain Operation Medusa to the public.

Courtesy 1 RCR BG.

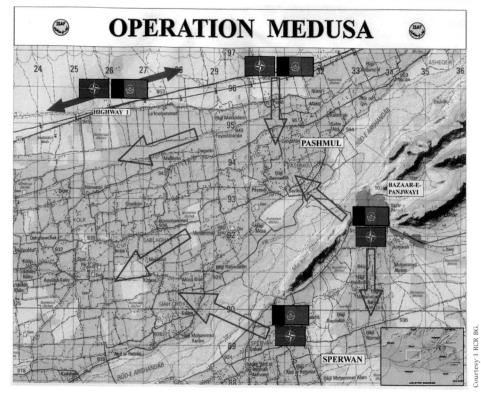

Courtesy 1 RCR BG.

A 7 Platoon LAV III provides security on Route Summit, October 2006.

The centre of Strong Point Centre prior to the attack. C/S 33C covers the northern approach of Route Summit.

Canadian Leopard 2 A6M tanks patrol along Route Summit, November 2006.

Members of TF 3-06 conduct a shura during Operation Baaz Tsuka, 18 December 2006.

Epilogue

The ongoing debate over Afghanistan is a difficult one. There are as many proponents declaring doom and gloom as there are those professing progress and victory. In the aftermath of Operation Medusa it becomes a quandary. Is the glass is half full or half empty? The Afghanistan Study Group claimed that 2007 was the deadliest year for coalition troops in Afghanistan since 2001. It noted that violence continued to escalate in 2008 with a 30 percent increase in violence nationwide.[1] In October 2008, two years after Operation Medusa, two high-ranking coalition officers stated that the war is not winnable. British Brigadier Mark Carleton-Smith, Britain's top military officer in Afghanistan, publicly said that people should "lower their expectations" with regards to how the conflict in Afghanistan would end. "We're not going to win this war," he bluntly stated. "It's about reducing it to a manageable level of insurgency that's not a strategic threat and can be managed by the Afghan Army." Several days later he was supported by the head of France's military, General Jean-Louis Georgelin, who commented frankly, "[the British officer] was saying that one cannot win this war militarily, that there is no military solution to the Afghan crisis and I totally share this feeling."[2] Their underlying message was reinforced several months later. In December, Norine MacDonald, president and lead field researcher of the International Council on Security and Development, formerly known as the Senlis Council, insisted, "the West is in genuine danger of losing Afghanistan."[3]

All of these assessments pale in light of announcements made by the vice president of the United States and the prime minister of Canada in March 2009. Joe Biden unambiguously stated, "We are not winning the war in Afghanistan," and Steven Harper declared, "We are not ever going to defeat the insurgents."[4] These assessments were not much different from the observations of the ISAF commander. In September 2009, American General Stanley McChrystal noted, "Eight years of individually successful kinetic actions have resulted in more violence."[5] A month later he acknowledged that the insurgency was growing. He concluded that success could not be taken for granted.[6] In fact, in November 2009, NATO conceded that 30 percent of Afghanistan was under strong Taliban leadership.[7] Other analysts declared that half of Afghanistan was either contested or controlled by the Taliban.[8] By the spring of 2010, declarations that the war was unwinnable and that negotiations with the Taliban should be considered no longer created a backlash of indignation. It was generally accepted as a reality and as a possible exit strategy for Western nations embroiled in Afghanistan.[9]

So the question must be asked: was Operation Medusa a wasted effort? Brigadier-General Fraser would argue that it was not. He noted that he had "no regrets about his decisions [and] at the end of the day, the measure of success was who won and who lost." Fraser unequivocally asserted, "We won, they lost."[10] Later he admitted, "It was one of the hardest things we've done for a very long time. Canada led the operation, NATO's biggest one ever, and successfully defeated the Taliban in this area. Canada did what was right and the cost was not insignificant."[11] Importantly, he professed, "Every life given here, every soldier that is wounded and will live for the rest of his life with scars, either physical or mental, has to understand that what he or she did here this summer and this fall meant something."[12]

Of course he was right. And it did mean something; as many proponents of success in Afghanistan have argued, Operation Medusa supported, if not invigorated, important advancements. By 7 September 2007, a year later, six million children were able to attend school. In Kandahar alone there were 4,000 community-based schools. In addition there were 9,000 teachers trained; literacy courses established for 6,400 people, including 5,400 women; 544 infrastructure projects completed in Kandahar (including construction of over 1,100 wells, 800 hand pumps, four large reservoirs, three water supply networks, 150 kilometres of new roads, four bridges, 50 kilometres of power lines, 10 transformers, 42 power generators, and 142 kilometres of irrigation systems); close to 6,000 kilometres of rehabilitated roads were completed; and 1.2 billion square metres of land was cleared of mines. Moreover, the coalition assisted with the election and employment of 400 local officials in Kandahar and is now training about 2,000 ANA soldiers per month.[13]

Equally important, according to senior political and military decision makers, was the fact that Operation Medusa was an important strategic and psychological victory. "Operation Medusa, in the south, was a near-conventional military operation initiated by Taliban insurgents who, quite mistakenly, believed that the newly arrived NATO forces would not fight. They were wrong, and they suffered a major tactical defeat, the effects of which significantly restricted their capabilities to mount a Spring Offensive in 2007,"[14] explained General Jones. Crucially, Operation Medusa, on the surface at any rate, demonstrated that NATO could and would fight.[15] Official NATO pronouncements declared, "NATO launched its largest ever combat operation, against a well-prepared and determined enemy. It was fought to the south west of Kandahar City, in the Panshwaye and Zhari Districts. It was here that the Taliban filtered in large numbers of insurgents in to first taken and then, far more significantly, hold the area. It was a trial of strength that will have a lasting effect both militarily and on the hearts and minds of the Afghan people."[16] Significantly, Afghan experts and analysts publicly recognized that Operation Medusa rescued Afghanistan from the tipping point.

A third, and equally significant, impact of Operation Medusa was that it signalled to allies and the Canadian public that the national peacekeeper myth was dead. Canada was once again prepared to deliberately send its sons and daughters into combat. In simplest terms, Canada reiterated its status, earned in blood and tears on so many foreign battlefields throughout its history, as a fighting nation. This was not missed by our allies. U.S. Secretary of State Condoleezza Rice stated, "They've [Taliban] learned a tough lesson that the Canadians are fierce fighters."[17] Similarly, Australian Prime Minister John Howard acknowledged, "Canada is carrying a very heavy burden in Afghanistan."[18]

And he was right. In 2006, Canada led in troop fatalities in Afghanistan as a percentage of troops deployed. Canada had 5.1 percent fatalities, the U.K. 3.6 percent, and the U.S. 2.5. When troop fatalities and wounded were factored, Canada had a 23.9 percent casualty rate compared to 18.3 and 14.3 for the U.K. and U.S. respectively. The European allies were not even close.[19]

Supporting Canada's contribution was also President Hamid Karzai who, in February 2007, told Canadian Foreign Affairs Minister Peter MacKay that "Canadians are putting their lives on the line to bring our [Afghanistan] country out of poverty and exploitation. They are coming here all the way from Canada with good in their hearts — and we are grateful."[20] He later addressed the Canadian Parliament and declared, "If the greatness of a life is measured in deeds done for others, then Canada's sons and daughters who have made the ultimate sacrifice can stand among the greatest of their generation. More than anyone else, Afghans very much understand that these sacrifices are for a great, good cause ... the cause of security for all and the cause of peace."[21]

Medusa was also a major watershed for the army. Not only was it NATO's first battle, but it also marked the first deliberate, major Canadian combat offensive operation since the Korean War. "Medusa had a significant psychological effect both on Taliban and us," offered intelligence officer, Captain Tim Button.[22] Despite endless Cold War exercises where umpires would designate casualties and take soldiers and occasionally leaders "out of play" temporarily, Medusa forced the army to face the reality of war — mass casualties and a mission that still had to be completed regardless of dead and wounded. From combat drills, equipment purchases and modifications, training regimes, and focus, as well as individual soldier and leader psychological preparation, the army has grown from its Afghan experience overall, but specifically from Operation Medusa. The army has proven to itself, and anyone who may have still held the Cold War mythology, that it is anything but a peacekeeping force.

But in the end, as always, the soldier's perspective drills down to the core of the issue. With regard to Operation Medusa, Master-Warrant Officer Keith Olstad said it best when he concluded, "It had to be done."[23]

NOTES

Introduction

1. Walter Laqueur, an internationally renowned expert on terrorism and insurgency, asserts that "terrorism constitutes the illegitimate use of force to achieve a political objective when innocent people are targeted." Benjamin Netanyahu, a former special operations soldier and prime minister of Israel, defined terrorism as "the deliberate and systemic assault on civilians to inspire fear for political ends." In a similar vein, Brian Jenkins stated, "Terrorism is the use or threatened use of force designed to bring about political change." Finally, scholar Michael Walzer explained, "Terrorism is the random killing of innocent people, in the hope of creating pervasive fear." He added, "The fear can serve many political purposes. Randomness and innocence are crucial elements in the definition."

   The American Federal Bureau of Investigation (FBI) definition states, "Terrorism is the unlawful use of force and violence against persons or property to intimidate or coerce a government, the civilian population, or any segment thereof, in furtherance of political or social objectives." The U.S. Departments of State and Defense define terrorism as "premeditated, politically motivated violence perpetrated against a noncombatant target by sub-national groups or clandestine state agents, usually intended to influence an audience." Within the context of NATO, terrorism is defined as "the unlawful use or threatened use of force or violence against individuals or property in an attempt to coerce or intimidate governments or societies to achieve political, religious or ideological objectives." See Barry Davies, *Terrorism: Inside a World Phenomenon* (London: Virgin, 2003), 14; Benjamin Netanyahu, *Fighting Terrorism: How Democracies Can Defeat the International Terrorist Network* (New York: Noonday Press, 1995), 8; Michael Walzer, "Terrorism and Just War," *Philosophia*, Vol 34, No. 1 (January 2006), 3; Roger W. Barnett, *Asymmetric Warfare: Today's Challenge to U.S. Military Power* (Washington, D.C.: Brassey's Inc, 2003), 16; John P. Holms, *Terrorism* (New York: Pinnacle Books, 2001), 20; and NATO Allied Administrative Publication 6, 2002, quoted in *Joint Doctrine & Concept Centre, Countering Terrorism: The UK Approach to the Military Contribution* (London: MOD, no date), 7.

2. UNSC Resolution 1368 recognized the inherent right of individual or collective self-defence in accordance with the UN Charter. It called on all states to work together urgently to bring to justice to the perpetrators, organizers, and sponsors of those terrorist attacks and stressed that those responsible for aiding, supporting, or harbouring the perpetrators, organizers, and sponsors of those acts would be held accountable. The resolution also expressed readiness to take all necessary steps to respond to the terrorist attacks of 11 September 2001 and to combat all forms of terrorism in accordance with its responsibilities under the Charter of the UN.

3. General Rick Hillier, *A Soldier First: Bullets, Bureaucrats and the Politics of War* (Toronto: HarperCollins, 2009), 475.

4. *Ibid.*, 488.

Chapter One

1. Quoted in United Kingdom, Parliament, House of Commons Library, International Affairs & Defence Section, Research Paper 01/72, 11 September 2001: the response, 31 October 2002, 17. *www.parliament.uk/commons/lib/re-search/rp2001/rp01-112.pdf*, accessed 7 March 2007.

The history between the Americans and Osama bin Laden and al Qaeda (AQ) was long-standing. They had tracked bin Laden from Sudan to Afghanistan. On 28 August 1998, the Americans were able to convince the Security Council to pass UN Security Council Resolution (UNSCR) 1193, which demanded that "Afghan factions … refrain from harboring and training terrorists and their organizations." UNSCR 214, passed on 8 December 1998, affirmed that the Security Council was "deeply disturbed by the continuing use of Afghan territory, especially areas controlled by the Taliban, for the sheltering and training of terrorists and the planning of terrorist acts" and reiterated that "the suppression of international terrorism is essential for the maintenance of international peace and security."

The Americans continued their UN offensive. On 15 October 1999, the U.S. secured the adoption of UNSCR 1267, which expressed concerns about the "continuing violations of international humanitarian law and of human rights [in Afghanistan], particularly discrimination against women and girls," as well as "the significant rise in the illicit production of opium." The resolution specifically criticized the Taliban for offering "safe haven to Osama bin Laden and to allow him and others associated with him to operate a network of terrorist training camps … and to use Afghanistan as a base from which to sponsor international terrorist operations." The Security Council demanded "that the Taliban turn over Osama bin Laden without further delay" so that he could be "effectively brought to justice." The council also instituted the same economic and financial sanctions on the Taliban regime that had recently been imposed by the United States. The Taliban failed to comply and on 12 October 2000, the AQ attacked the USS *Cole* in the harbour at Aden, killing 17 U.S. sailors and wounding 39 more. To exacerbate the looming showdown, bin Laden took full credit for the operation, prompting the Security Council to pass UNSCR 1333 on 19 December 2000. This resolution reaffirmed the charges made a year earlier and added the stipulation that the Taliban were to ensure the closing "of all camps where terrorists are trained." In addition, economic sanctions were strengthened, Taliban offices were to be closed in the territory of member states, landing rights for Afghan national airways were revoked, and all assets linked to Osama bin Laden and al Qaeda were frozen.

Once again the Taliban regime did nothing. As a result, yet another UNSCR was passed on 30 July 2001, which described "the situation in Afghanistan ... as a threat to international peace and security in the region." In the weeks leading up to 9/11, Afghanistan had already been identified as a major threat centre for American national interest. See *United Nations Security Council Resolution 1193*, 28 August 1998; *Resolution 1214*, 8 December 1998; *Resolution 1267*, 15 October 1999; *Resolution 1333*, 19 December 2000; *Resolution 1363*, 30 July 2001; Ahmed Rashid, *Taliban: Militant Islam, Oil and Fundamentalism in Central Asia* (New Haven, CT: Yale University Press, 2001), 80; Daniel Benjamin and Steven Simon, *The Age of Sacred Terror* (New York: Random House, 2002), xiii and 289. See also Steve Coll, *Ghost Wars: The Secret History of the CIA, Afghanistan and bin Laden from the Soviet Invasion to September 10, 2001* (New York: Penguin Books, 2004) for a comprehensive account of the U.S./bin Laden/AQ interrelationship.

2. North Atlantic Council Statement, 12 September 2001, Press Release (2001)124, *www.nato.int/docu/pr/2001/p01-124e.htm*, accessed 7 March 2007; and NATO, *NATO Handbook* (Brussels: NATO Office of Information and Press, 1995), 232.

3. Statement by NATO Secretary General Lord Robertson, 4 October 2001, *www.nato.int/docu/speech/2001/s011004a.htm*, accessed 7 March 2007. See also Tom Lansford, *All for One: Terrorism, NATO, and the United States* (Farnham, U.K.: Ashgate Publishing, 2002), 126.

4. See *United Nations Security Council Resolutions 1368*, 12 September 2001 and *UNSCR 1373*, 28 September 2001.

5. See Janice Gross Stein and Eugene Lange, *The Unexpected War: Canada in Kandahar* (Toronto: Viking Canada, 2007), 2–34.

6. "Chrétien: Canadian Troops 'Will Do Canada Proud,'" 7 October 2001, *www.ctv.ca/servlet/ArticleNews/story/CTVNews/1025062429054_20471629*, accessed 7 October 2001.

7. Canada, *How Are We Doing in Afghanistan?* Report of the Standing Senate Committee on National Security and Defence," June 2008, 1.

8. The CDS also articulated a series of CDS objectives:

    a. forces committed to the coalition will be employed in the attainment of coalition and national objectives;

    b. forces offered by the GoC but not yet requested by the U.S. will be prepared and available for deployment; and

    c. employment of CF will be in accordance with Canadian national laws.

The CDS retained full command throughout. The CDS assigned operational command (OPCOM) of the four components of the Operation Apollo contribution to the commander Canadian Joint Task Force Southwest Asia (JTFSWA), who also had authority to assign operational control (OPCON) of those forces to coalition commanders as required within the U.S. CENTCOM AOR to achieve coalition and national objectives. The role of the Canadian JTFSWA commander was that of Canada's senior national commander-in-theatre of Operation Apollo. He was responsible for supervising the operational readiness, administration, and discipline of Canadian task groups and elements deployed to Operation Apollo, as well as to monitor operations of task groups on behalf of CDS assigned under OPCON coalition commanders. The Canadian commitment also included a special operations task force from JTF 2.

9. The multi-national forces took control of Kandahar on 7 December 2001. American efforts then shifted to tracking down Osama bin Laden and his top AQ leadership. Canadian air, sea, and SOF elements remained to support the ongoing American and Coalition force efforts.

10. *United Nations Security Council Resolutions 1378*, 14 November 2001.

11. The first of the ISAF troops deployed to Kabul on 22 December 2001.

12. Lieutenant-Colonel Pat Stogran was the commanding officer. During their six months in Afghanistan, 3 PPCLI Battle Group performed tasks ranging from airfield security to combat operations.

13. Canada, *Canadian Forces in Afghanistan*, Report of the Standing Committee on National Defence, June 2007, 39.

14. John McCallum, "Stepping Up to the Plate," *Washington Times*, 31 July 2003.

15. Lieutenant-General Rick Hillier, presentation at the Army Strategic Planning Session 7, Cornwall, Ontario, 29 November 2003.

16. The International Security Assistance Force (ISAF) is a United Nations-mandated operation, but is NATO-led. It was authorized by United Nations Security Council Resolutions (UNSCRs) 1386, 1413, 1444, and 1510. UNSCR 1386 (20 December 2001), as well as UNSCR 1413, authorize ISAF to operate under Chapter VII of the UN Charter (peace-enforcing). Furthermore, under UNSCR 1444 (27 November 2002) the role of ISAF remained to assist in the maintenance of security and to help the Afghan Transitional Authority (Afghan TA) and the initial activities of the United Nations in Kabul and its environs — nowhere else. However, UNSCR 1510 (13 October 2003) authorized the expansion of the ISAF mandate beyond the original provision of security in the Kabul area into the rest of Afghanistan. The first ISAF troops deployed as a multi-national force (without Canadian participation) initially under British command on 4 January 2002.

17. On 9 October 2004, Afghanistan held presidential elections. Hamid Karzai won 55.4 percent of the popular vote and became president. More than 10 million Afghans registered to vote. Parliamentary and provincial council elections were held on 18 September 2005 and 6.8 million Afghans participated. On 19 December 2005 the national Assembly, composed of 249 members of the Wolesi Jirga (lower house) — all elected — and 102 members of the Meshrano Jirga (upper house) — some appointed — stood up. *Canada's Mission in Afghanistan: Measuring Progress*, Report to Parliament, February 2007, 11.

18. The last Canadian material assets were moved and shipped to Kandahar on 29 November 2005, and Camp Julien, the Canadian base in Kabul, was officially handed over to the Afghan Ministry of Defence.

19. On 17 May 2006, Parliament voted to extend the Canadian military mission in Kandahar Province, as well as the work of the PRT, until February 2009.

20. *Managing Turmoil: The Need to Upgrade Canadian Foreign Aid and Military Strength to Deal with Massive Change*, an Interim Report of the Standing Senate Committee on National Security and Defence, October 2006, 150. See also Michelle Parker, "Programming Development Funds to Support a Counterinsurgency: A Case Study of Nangarhar, Afghanistan in 2006," *Case Studies in National Security Transformation*, Number 10, nd, 2.

21. *Managing Turmoil: The Need to Upgrade Canadian Foreign Aid and Military Strength to Deal with Massive Change*, an Interim Report of the Standing Senate Committee on National Security and Defence, October 2006, 149. The PRT in Kandahar focused on three major areas: good governance, security sector reform (including providing training and equipment to Afghan police), and reconstruction and development.

22. General Rick Hillier, "Exporting Stability," *Vanguard*, February/March 2006, 30.

23. Daniel Leblanc, "JTF 2 to Hunt Al-Qaeda," *Globe and Mail*, 15 July 2005, A1. The attacks that prompted Hillier's comments occurred on 7 July 2005 (7/7) when a number of British Muslims carried out a series of coordinated suicide-bomb attacks on London's public transportation system during the morning rush hour. They killed 52 people and injured approximately 700. At 0850 hours, three detonations were triggered within 50 seconds of each other on three London subway trains. A fourth explosion occurred nearly an hour later, at 0947 hours on a bus in Tavistock Square. The suicide bombings represented the largest and deadliest terrorist attack on London's transit system. The attacks were allegedly motivated by Britain's involvement in the Iraq War and Afghanistan.

24. Rory Leishman, "Fighting Taliban Protects Canada," *London Free Press*, 2 January 2007, A6.

25. Paul Koring, "More Troops at Risk, General Warns. Ottawa says CF-18s ready for Afghanistan," *Globe and Mail*. The MND, Gordon O'Connor, also asserted, "Our CF are in Afghanistan because it is in our national interest because we have the responsibility to take a leadership role in world affairs and because Afghans need us and

want us to help them." *Canadian Forces in Afghanistan*, Report of the Standing Committee on National Defence, June 2007, 40.

26. NATO took control of ISAF in 2003. Since then it has expanded: to the north in 2004 (Stage I), to the west in 2005 (Stage II), and the plan to move to the south (Stage III) transpired in 2005/2006.

27. *Canadian Forces in Afghanistan*, Report of the Standing Committee on National Defence, June 2007, 11.

28. *Ibid.*, 6. While the intent to assist others was certainly there, we should not fool ourselves into believing the decision to deploy forces in a combat role in Afghanistan was completely altruistic. In keeping with the "supporting allies" theme, the Canadian engagement in Afghanistan has positively affected our relationship with the U.S. It is no coincidence that many of the issues that remained insoluble (e.g., mad cow disease, NAFTA, softwood lumber, and border issues) quietly disappeared. As one senior Canadian general officer stated, "It [combat role in Afghanistan] has resulted in a 'sea change in the [U.S./Canadian] relationship.'"

29. Sally Armstrong, "Honour Roll 2006: Envoy Extraordinary," *Maclean's*, 27 June 2006, *www.macleans.ca/culture/people/article.isp? content_20060701_129993_12993*, accessed 18 July 2006.

30. Canadian High Commission, "Cause for Celebration on 'Independence Day,'" *Canada Focus*, 21 September 2007, 1.

31. "Canadian Forces Operations in Afghanistan," DND Backgrounder, 15 May 2007. The Canadian efforts were in support of the internationally supported Afghanistan Compact, which was developed in London, 31 January to 1 February 2006. The Compact commits international community (more than 60 countries and international organizations) along with the GoA and the UN to achieve progress in three critical and interrelated areas of activity for the period 2006–11: security; governance, including rule of law, human rights, and tackling corruption; and economic and social development. The Afghan Compact aimed to: triple the Afghan army to 70,000 troops; disband all illegal militias by 2007; reduce by 70 percent the amount of land made unusable by land mines by 2010; reduce the number of people living on less than $1 a day by

3 percent per year and the proportion of those who are hungry by 5 percent per year; create functioning justice institutions in every province by end of 2010, including prisons with separate facilities for women and juveniles; upgrade the country's main ring road, central to government plans to revive Afghanistan's historic role as a land bridge between Central and South Asia; bring electricity to 65 percent of urban homes and 25 percent of rural homes by the end of 2010; enroll 60 percent of girls and 75 percent of boys in primary school by 2010.

32. Canada, *How Are We doing in Afghanistan?*, 1. The Standing Committee set the following benchmarks for success:

    1. a government that is able to provide for the security and safety of its citizens;
    2. a citizenry that is fed and sheltered in an adequate manner;
    3. significant improvements to the infrastructure such as wells, roads, and schools;
    4. basic health services;
    5. education that is universally available to both genders;
    6. steps are well advanced in the development of a democratic process in the province; and
    7. a growing and diversified economy that does not rely on the drug trade.

    See Canada, *Managing Turmoil*, 34. Retired Major-General Lewis MacKenzie, the first commander of United Nations peacekeeping forces in Sarajevo, summarized the aim of the mission as, "to leave Afghanistan as quickly as humanly possible — having turned the security of the country over to competent Afghan military and police forces controlled in their efforts by a democratically elected national government."

33. Hillier, "Exporting Stability," 30.

34. The 1 PPCLI Battle Group (BG) consisted of 1 PPCLI, a tactical unmanned aerial vehicle (TUAV) troop, an HSS company, a forward support group (FSG), and the Kandahar Provincial

Reconstruction team (PRT). Hope stated that he chose the name Orion to give everyone a common identifier. "I chose Orion from the constellation — representing the mythical Greek hunter of mountain beasts — that I knew blessed the Afghan skies, so that our soldiers might look up and seeing it, feel part of a larger entity, enduring and meaningful." Ian Hope, "Reflections on Afghanistan: Commanding Task Force Orion," in B. Horn, ed., *In Harm's Way. The Buck Stops Here: Senior Officers on Operations* (Kingston: CDA Press, 2007), 212. See also Lieutenant-Colonel Ian Hope, *Dancing with the Dushman: Command Imperatives for the Counter-Insurgency Fight in Afghanistan* (Kingston: CDA Press, 2008).

35. "1st Battalion Princess Patricia's Canadian Light Infantry Battle Group (Task Force Orion) — Operational Summary," 12 August 2006; and Ian Hope, "Reflections on Afghanistan: Commanding Task Force Orion," in B. Horn, ed., *In Harm's Way. The Buck Stops Here: Senior Officers on Operations* (Kingston: CDA Press, 2007), 212. Hope stated, "Our tasks were multifarious, divided into three broad categories: governance, security and reconstruction."

Chapter Two

1. Lieutenant-Colonel Ian Hope, *Dancing with the Dushman: Command Imperatives for the Counter-Insurgency Fight in Afghanistan* (Kingston: CDA Press, 2008), 153.

2. Quoted in Chris Wattie, *Contact Charlie: The Canadian Army, The Taliban and the Battle that Saved Afghanistan* (Toronto: Key Porter Books, 2008), 53.

3. On 31 July 2006, the Task Force reverted to operational command of ISAF.

4. The change in leadership was quickly apparent to Hope. He explained, "Under Operation Enduring Freedom there was a prevailing philosophy of 'mission command' with echelons of headquarters pushing resources to the commander in the fight, and asking him what more he needed. There was never second-guessing or micro-

management of the battalion's battles. Under ISAF the philosophy was reverting to one of tight control of everything by general officers many hundreds of kilometers away." Hope, *Dancing with the Dushman*, 15.

5. Despite all of the sensors and HUMINT, Hope noted that he "never had more than 20 percent of the information. Most often not even that much." Lieutenant-Colonel Ian Hope, presentation — Canadian Infantry Association Annual General Meeting, 25 May 2007.

6. Ian Hope, "Reflections on Afghanistan: Commanding Task Force Orion," in B. Horn, ed., *In Harm's Way. The Buck Stops Here: Senior Officers on Operations* (Kingston: CDA Press, 2007), 216–17.

7. Lieutenant-Colonel Ian Hope, presentation — Canadian Infantry Association Annual General Meeting, 25 May 2007.

8. Captain Kevin Barry, TF Orion QRF Commander, 1 CMBG briefing, 22 January 2007.

9. Lieutenant-Colonel Shane Schreiber, Operations Officer MNB HQ, 1 CMBG briefing, 22 January 2007.

10. "Biggest Cdn/U.K./U.S. Operation Since Korea," *The Canadian Army News*, 28 August 2006, *www.army.forces.gc.ca/land-terre/news-nouvelles/story-reportage-eng.asp?id=1219*, accessed 14 June 2010.

11. *Ibid.*

12. The Senlis Council, *Canada in Kandahar: No Peace to Keep. A Case Study of the Military Coalitions in Southern Afghanistan*, London, June 2006, v.

13. *Ibid.*, xi.

14. *Ibid.*, 31.

15. "Brigade and Battle Group Operations — Kandahar and Helmand — July 2006," CO's PPT presentation. ANSF consisted of the ANA, Afghan National Police (ANP) and border forces.

16. Quoted in Wattie, 209.

17. Captain Andrew Charchuk, "'Contact C' A Forward Observation Officer with Task Force Orion," *The Canadian Army Journal*, Vol 10.2, Summer 2007, 25. The RPG 29 is a lightweight (11.5 kg) and concealable weapon. It has a range of 800 metres and can penetrate more than 750 millimetres of armour, 1.5 metres of reinforced concrete or brick, and 3.7 metres of logs and earth.

18. Christie Blatchford, *Fifteen Days: Stories of Bravery, Friendship, Life and Death from Inside the New Canadian Army* (Toronto: Doubleday Canada, 2007), 13.

19. Lieutenant-Colonel Shane Schreiber, Operations Officer MNB HQ, 1 CMBG briefing, 22 January 2007.

20. Hope, *Dancing with the Dushman*, 16.

21. Schreiber, 1 CMBG briefing, 22 January 2007.

22. *Ibid.*

23. Hope, *Dancing with the Dushman*, 5.

24. Master-Corporal Matthew Parsons, interview with author, 24 January 2007.

25. Quoted in Wattie, 214.

26. Lieutenant-Colonel Ian Hope, Presentation — Canadian Infantry Association Annual General Meeting, 25 May 2007.

27. Terry Pedwell, "Taliban 'Were Too Organized,'" *Canadian Press*, 4 August 2006.

28. Sergeant Patrick Towers, interview with author, 24 January 2007.

29. Brigadier-General David Fraser, interview with author 21 October 2006. The interview has been captured in full in Brigadier-General David Fraser, "No Small Victory: Insights of the Commander of Combined Task Force Aegis on Operation Medusa," in Colonel Bernd Horn, ed., *In Harm's Ways. The Buck Stops Here: Operational Perspectives of Senior Military Leaders* (Kingston: CDA Press, 2007), 243–56.

30. Confidential Interview, 10 July 2008.

31. Hope, *Dancing with the Dushman*, 9.

32. *Ibid.*, 13.

33. *Ibid.*, 6.

34. *Ibid.*, 13.

35. *Ibid.*, 15–16.

36. Terry Pedwell, "Deadly Day for Troops," *Kingston Whig-Standard*, 4 August 2006, 9.

37. Brigadier-General David Fraser, interview with author 21 October 2006. During their tour 1 PPCLI BG conducted: 128 Shuras/ leadership engagements; 29 operations; 23 combined operations with ANSF; 646 total patrols; and 291 joint patrols with ANSF. They

clocked 1,700,000 kilometres of driving. They also participated in 15 intensive firefights and 100+ troops in contact (TICs). They were the target of 67 Small arms attacks; 59 RPG attacks; 33 rocket attacks; 16 mortar attacks; and 25 IED attacks. They captured 39 detainees, inflicted four confirmed and 181 estimated enemy wounded in action (WIA), and 26 confirmed and 213 estimated enemy killed in action (KIA). They themselves suffered 10 percent casualties — 19 KIA and 76 WIA. "1st Battalion Princess Patricia's Canadian Light Infantry Battle Group (Task Force Orion) — Operational Summary," 12 August 2006.

38. Brigadier-General David Fraser, interview with author, 21 October 2006.
39. Blatchford, 250.
40. Brigadier-General David Fraser, interview with author, 21 October 2006.
41. This refers to the Maoist model of insurgency: Phase 1 — Strategic Defence: focus on survival and building support. Bases are established, local leaders are recruited, cellular networks and parallel governments created; Phase 2 — Strategic Stalemate: guerilla warfare ensues. Insurgents focus on separating population from government; Phase 3 – Strategic Offensive: Insurgents feel they have superior strength and move to conventional operations to destroy government capability.
42. Brigadier-General David Fraser, interview with author, 21 October 2006.
43. *Ibid.*
44. *Ibid.*
45. Blatchford, 251.

Chapter Three

1. Christie Blatchford, *Fifteen Days* (Toronto: Doubleday Canada, 2007), 251.
2. One reporter noted, "NATO is hoping to bring a new strategy to dealing with the Taliban rebellion: establishing bases rather than

chasing militants, and is also hoping to win the support of local people by creating secure zones where development can take place. But questions remain whether they can quell the violence enough to allow aid workers to get to work in a lawless and impoverished region [Kandahar Province] where about a quarter of Afghanistan's huge opium crop is grown, and the narcotics trade fuels the insurgency." Fisnik Abrashi, "NATO Takes Command in Afghanistan," *Kingston Whig-Standard*, 31 July 2006, 10.

3. Brigadier-General David Fraser, presentation — Canadian Infantry Association Annual General Meeting, 25 May 2007.

4. Brigadier-General David Fraser, interview with author, 21 October 2006. Lieutenant-Colonel Schreiber explained that there were five challenges that faced the MNB/ISAF: the image of the ANP; the will of the ANA; the inability of the people to protect themselves; the information operations capability of the Taliban; and the insoluble issue of Pashtunwali. Lieutenant-Colonel Shane Schreiber, interview with author, 22 October 2006.

5. Brigadier-General David Fraser, interview with author, 21 October 2006.

6. Lieutenant-Colonel Peter Williams, interview with author, 22 October 2006. Williams added, "There was a substantial conventional threat in the vicinity of the Panjwayi area west of Kandahar City, to the point that we thought that this threatened the security of the city and the freedom to move to Highway Number 1 and the city might be isolated and the Taliban could claim a great IO [information operations] victory."

7. Captain C. Purdy, interview with author, 17 October 2006.

8. Lieutenant-Colonel Shane Schreiber, interview with author, 18 October 2006.

9. *Ibid.*

10. Brigadier-General David Fraser, interview with author, 21 October 2006.

11. *Ibid.*

12. Lieutenant-Colonel Shane Schreiber interview with author, 18 October 2006. Schreiber noted, "And a very sophisticated C2 node.

Somebody actually reinforcing, directing reinforcements to exact positions. Somebody actually controlling the battle."

13. Lieutenant-Colonel Shane Schreiber, ACOS, Multi-National Brigade HQ, 1 CMBG briefing, 22 January 2007.

14. Memo, Director Army Training to Commander Land Force Development Training System, "Tactical Reconnaissance Report — Training Assessment OP Archer Rotation 3," 21 September 2006, 3. SPG refers to the Soviet designation Stankovyy Protivotankovyy Granatamet or, literally translated, mounted anti-tank grenade launcher. In NATO terminology it refers to an anti-tank recoilless rifle.

15. General Hillier explained in an interview, "The challenge is that marijuana plants absorb energy, heat very readily. It's very difficult to penetrate them with thermal devices … And as a result you really have to be careful that the Taliban don't dodge in and out of those marijuana forests. We tried burning them with white phosphorous — it didn't work. We tried burning them with diesel — it didn't work. The plants are so full of water right now … that we simply couldn't burn them. A couple of brown plants on the edges of some of those [forests] did catch on fire. But a section of soldiers that was downwind from that had some ill effects and decided that was probably not the right course of action." "Canada Troops Battle 10-Foot Afghan Marijuana Plants," *cnn.com*, *www.cnn.com/2006/WORLD/Americas/10/12/ Canada.troops.marijuana.reut/index.html*, accessed 13 October 2006.

16. Memo, Director Army Training to Commander Land Force Development Training System, "Tactical Reconnaissance Report — Training Assessment OP Archer Rotation 3," 21 September 2006, 3.

17. Captain C. Purdy, interview with author, 17 October 2006.

18. Brigadier-General David Fraser, interview with author, 21 October 2006.

19. Brigadier-General David Fraser, interview with author, 22 October 2006.

20. Brigadier-General David Fraser, interview with author, 21 October 2006.

21. Janice Gross Stein, *The Unexpected War: Canada in Kandahar* (Toronto: Viking, 2007), 219.

22. Brigadier-General David Fraser, interview with author, 21 October 2006.

23. Donald McArthur, "Canadian Troops Pressed Ahead on Operation Medusa," *Canada.com*, 6 September 2006, *www.canada.com/components/ print.aspx?id=5e81f24-dd05-4eb6-88c1-bbd5e09251f8&k=50060*, accessed 10 September 2006.

24. General Rick Hillier, *A Soldier First: Bullets, Bureaucrats and the Politics of War* (Toronto: HarperCollins, 2009), 475–76. In the aftermath of Operation Medusa, Hillier told his peers, "Canada feels like we've been abandoned by our allies in the Kandahar province fight."

25. FOB Martello was built on the Tarin Kowt Road on the way to the Dutch AO in the province of Uruzgan by the 1 PPCLI Battle Group, in order to secure the northern part of Kandahar Province to support NATO's expansion into that province.

26. Brigadier-General David Fraser, interview with author, 21 October 2006. The interview has been captured in full in Brigadier-General David Fraser, "No Small Victory: Insights of the Commander of Combined Task Force Aegis on Operation Medusa," in Colonel Bernd Horn, ed., *In Harm's Ways. The Buck Stops Here: Operational Perspectives of Senior Military Leaders* (Kingston: CDA Press, 2007), 243–56. Lieutenant-Colonel Schreiber noted, "It's the enablers that win the fight."

27. Situation Briefing, Senior CF officer, NDHQ, 5 June 2007. A senior NATO commander lamented on 6 June 2007, "The European perception is that there is an ISAF mission and an OEF mission. According to European politicians ISAF does stabilization and OEF fights." General Hillier recalled, "The NATO Secretary-General went around to the members of the alliance constantly to beg two more helicopters or five hundred more troops or something else for Afghanistan, in an alliance that has millions of soldiers and thousands of helicopters. It was embarrassing." Hillier, *A Soldier First*, 477.

28. Brigadier-General David Fraser, interview with author, 21 October 2006. Because of the inability of NATO countries to "pony up" troops, Fraser had to become creative. He explained, "I had to constitute the appropriate force because I was short of soldiers. As a result, the British and the Dutch sent troops that were able to take over

certain outposts and garrisons, which in turn freed up the Canadian troops from TF 3-06 (i.e., 1 RCR Battle Group) so that they could concentrate themselves in Pashmul to conduct the actual offensive. In addition, I asked Task Force 31 (American Special Forces) if they could go and conduct operations to our southwest near Sperwan. That way I could concentrate my forces on the main effort in the Pashmul area."

29. Steven Chase and Campbell Clark, "Hillier: Torture Claims were 'Ludicrous,' Lacking in Substance," *Globe and Mail*, 26 November 2009, A7.

30. Lieutenant-Colonel Shane Schreiber interview with author, 18 October 2006.

Chapter Four

1. The 1 RCR/1 PPCLI RIP occurred from 24 July to 24 August 2006.

2. Commander's Entry, TF 3-06 War Diary, 19–31 August 2006.

3. Colonel Omer Lavoie, "Leadership in Combat and RMC's Role," article for RCR ROIC Candidates, 9–10 April 2010, Petawawa.

4. Major Mike Wright, interview with author, 13 October 2006.

5. Warrant Officer Mike Jackson, interview with author, 13 October 2006.

6. Major Mike Wright, interview with author, 13 October 2006.

7. Warrant Officer Mike Jackson, interview with author, 13 October 2006.

8. *Ibid*.

9. Captain Mike Leaky, interview with author, 13 October 2006.

10. Warrant Officer Mike Jackson, interview with author, 13 October 2006.

11. Major Mike Wright, interview with author, 13 October 2006.

12. Details of TF 3-06 operations are from an amalgam of extracts from the BG War Diary and operations documents, interviews, and press releases.

13. The idea was that once the enemy had been heavily reduced, through the sustained employment of joint fires, they would be forced to withdraw using their exfiltration routes to the south near Siah Choy,

where they would be interdicted by SOF elements and completely destroyed. The manoeuvre was initiated earlier than planned because of the window of availability for key enablers such as the Predator Unmanned Aerial Vehicle (UAV) that were required for Operation Mountain Fury in Regional Command East (RC [E]), which was running concurrently with Operation Medusa. Memo, Director Army Training to Commander Land Force Development Training System, "Tactical Reconnaissance Report — Training Assessment OP Archer Rotation 3," 21 September 2006, 4.

14. "H-Hour" is the designated time given for coordination of movement and fires for all engaged forces for any given operation.

15. Captain Rob Carey, interview with author, 16 October 2006.

16. Major Matthew Sprague, interview with author, 19 November 2007.

17. TF Kandahar narratives, 2 September 2006.

18. Lieutenant-Colonel Omer Lavoie, interview with author, 8 October 2006.

19. As quoted in Adam Day, "Operation Medusa: The Battle for Panjwai. Part I, The Charge of Charles Company," *Legion Magazine*, September/October 2007, *www.legionmagazine.com/features/militarymatters/07-09.asp*, accessed 19 November 2007.

20. Major Greg Ivey, interview with author, 17 October 2006.

21. *Ibid.* Ivey noted, "We suffered through ammunition re-supply issues just like you read about in the history books in Korea and World War II. Chinook helicopters were coming down dropping emergency loads of ammo and trucks were unloading rounds behind the guns. There were just piles and piles of 155mm ammunition casings from rounds going down range."

22. Confidential interview with SOF combat controller team member, 12 May 2007.

23. Lieutenant-Colonel Omer Lavoie, interview with author, 8 October 2006. Major Ivey noted, "The 25mm cannon worked out extremely well for us. It is an outstanding target marker and you don't need to be a FOO to be doing it. The infantry section for example, with Charles company, would pick up a target, if the FOO had a difficult time getting eyes on quickly, and there was nothing better than

seeing a 25mm burst going down range into that area. The FOO could get then get the eyes of the pilot onto it quite quickly, especially at night because of the IR [infra-red] capabilities." Major Greg Ivey, interview with author, 17 October 2006. See also John Conrad, *What the Thunder Said* (Toronto: Dundurn Press, 2009), 199–22.

24. Major Greg Ivey, interview with author, 17 October 2006.
25. *Ibid.*
26. Major Matthew Sprague, interview with author, 19 November 2007.
27. The school was built in 2004 with funds from the U.S. Commander's Emergency Reconstruction Program (CERP).
28. As quoted in Day, "Operation Medusa: The Battle for Panjwai," Part I.

Chapter Five

1. Major Matthew Sprague, interview with author, 19 November 2007.
2. Lieutenant-Colonel Shane Schreiber interview with author, 18 October 2006.
3. *Ibid.*
4. *Ibid.*
5. *Ibid.*
6. Major Matthew Sprague, interview with author, 19 November 2007.
7. The CO remembered, "I was struck that morning by the sheer outward confidence in the plan displayed by the leadership of the BG, despite the fact that for most of them it was their first time experiencing a combat engagement. I am certain many of my officers shared the same misgivings I had. There was certainly huge risk in some areas of the plan, especially if we failed to surprise the enemy." Colonel Omer Lavoie, "Leadership in Combat and RMC's Role," article for RCR ROIC candidates, 9–10 April 2010, Petawawa.
8. Major Greg Ivey, interview with author, 17 October 2006.
9. Major Matthew Sprague, interview with author, 19 November 2007.
10. Christie Blatchford, "Did He Abandon His Troops?" *Globe and Mail*, 29 December 2006, *www.theglobeandmail.com/servlet/story/ RTGAM.20061229.wxafghan-blatch29B*, accessed 30 December 2006.

11. Lieutenant Jeremy Hiltz, interview with author, 16 October 2006.

12. Major Matthew Sprague, interview with author, 19 November 2007.

13. Lieutenant Jeremy Hiltz, interview with author, 16 October 2006.

14. Adam Day, "Operation Medusa: The Battle For Panjwai, Part 2; Death in a Free Fire Zone," *Legion Magazine*, 1 November 2007, *www.legionmagazine.com/en/index.php/2007/11/operation-medusa-the-battle-for-panjwai-2*, accessed 8 July 2008.

15. Mitch Potter, "The Story of C Company," *Toronto Star*, 30 September 2006, *www.thestar.com/afghanistan/article/106992*, accessed 27 October 2006.

16. Corporal Justin Young, interview with author, 14 October 2006.

17. Lieutenant Jeremy Hiltz, interview with author, 16 October 2006.

18. Potter, "The Story of C Company."

19. Master-Corporal J. O'Neil, interview with author, 18 October 2006.

20. Corporal Sean Teal, interview with author, 14 October 2006.

21. Potter, "The Story of C Company."

22. Day, "Death in a Free Fire Zone."

23. Private Mike O'Rourke, interview with author, 14 October 2006.

24. Corporal Gary Reid, interview with author, 14 October 2006.

25. Private Mike O'Rourke, interview with author, 14 October 2006.

26. *Ibid.*

27. Niefer was later awarded the Military Medal of Valour.

28. Lieutenant Jeremy Hiltz, interview with author, 16 October 2006.

29. Sergeant Donovan Crawford, interview with author, 14 October 2006.

30. Lieutenant Ray Corby, interview with author, 14 October 2006.

31. Lieutenant Jeremy Hiltz, interview with author, 16 October 2006.

32. Day, "Death in a Free Fire Zone."

33. Private Mike O'Rourke, interview with author, 14 October 2006.

34. Potter, "The Story of C Company."

35. To this date there is no explanation. Two theories exist. One: it was a dud. Two: once the bomb fell off its GPS (global positioning system) track the arming device shut-off. Sprague opined, "We had lots of bad luck that day, but we also had lots of good luck as well." The aircraft has also been both described as a French Mirage and an American aircraft of unknown type.

36. Lieutenant Jeremy Hiltz, interview with author, 16 October 2006.

37. Lieutenant J. Bules, interview with author, 20 October 2006.

38. Confidential interview, 8 July 2008.

39. *Ibid.*

40. Major Matthew Sprague, interview with author, 19 November 2007.

41. Captain Rob Carey, interview with author, 16 October 2006.

42. *Ibid.*

43. Sergeant Jamie Walsh, interview with author, 14 October 2006.

44. Confidential interview, 8 July 2008.

45. Sergeant Jamie Walsh, interview with author, 14 October 2006.

46. Lieutenant Jeremy Hiltz, interview with author, 16 October 2006.

47. Lieutenant J. Bules, interview with author, 20 October 2006.

48. *Ibid.*

49. Major Greg Ivey, interview with author, 17 October 2006. Ivey praised the FOO, "And kudos to them because they did an outstanding job. They were able to pull back. They leaguered up on the Arghandab River to consolidate and do their casualty evacuation. So it was quite a day."

50. Master-Corporal J. O'Neil, interview with author, 18 October 2006.

51. Major Matthew Sprague, interview with author, 19 November 2007.

52. Quoted in Blatchford, 256.

53. Potter, "The Story of C Company."

54. Major Greg Ivey, interview with author, 17 October 2006.

55. Lieutenant-Colonel Shane Schreiber, interview with author, 18 October 2006.

56. Lieutenant Jeremy Hiltz, interview with author, 16 October 2006.

57. *Ibid.*

Chapter Six

1. Captain Ryan Jurkoskie, from TF Orion, saw the problem in a different light. He stated, "I felt that we left an unresolved situation for other people to deal with … Op Medusa should have been our battle group, we knew the battle space, we knew the fucking area,

we'd been patrolling through there day in and day out, decisions were made again for all the right reasons but tactically I think, anyways in my opinion, we were too dogmatic in the ingress and egress of our troops and the timelines associated with it rather than tactical fighting and where we had a two month learning curve prior to our fist firefight, we had two months to shake ourselves out. Their first firefight was in their RIP [relief in place], like holy fuck." Interview with author, 24 January 2007.

2. Interview with members of 7 Platoon, 14 October 2006.

3. Christie Blatchford, "Did He Abandon His Troops?" *Globe and Mail*, 29 December 2006, *www.theglobeandmail.com/servlet/story/RTGAM.20061229.wxafghan-blatch29B*, accessed 30 December 2006.

4. Quoted in Adam Day, "Operation Medusa: The Battle For Panjwai, Part 2; Death in a Free Fire Zone," *Legion Magazine*, 1 November 2007, *www.legionmagazine.com/en/index.php/2007/11/operation-medusa-the-battle-for-panjwai-2*, accessed 8 July 2008.

5. Master Warrant Officer Keith Olstad, interview with author, 11 January 2009.

6. Captain C. Purdy, interview with author, 17 October 2006.

7. *Ibid.*

8. Quoted in Adam Day, *Witness to War* (Ottawa: CDA Press/Magic Light Publishing, in press 2009), draft manuscript. Quote is based on a confidential interview.

9. Chief Warrant Officer Bob Girouard, interview with author, 15 October 2006. RSM Girouard was killed by a suicide vehicle EID on 27 November 2006. One sergeant revealed, "I knew that was going to happen that way. People did not take the enemy as serious as they should have. They went in too cocky." One of the SOF members who manned an OP on Ma'Sūm Ghar noted, "On 3 September when the RCR guys were going in, we radioed to our headquarters and told them we didn't think it was a good idea. The AC-130 overhead was reporting lots of guys [enemy] in the area. Also, we hadn't hit all the objectives effectively." He stated that it was no surprise that the Taliban was not fighting back. As he explained, "You can't fight LAVs and aircraft at a distance with RPGs." Confidential interviews, 8 July 2008.

10. Lieutenant-Colonel Omer Lavoie, interview with author, 8 October 2006.

11. Lieutenant-Colonel Omer Lavoie, letter to author, 25 May 2007.

12. Lieutenant-Colonel Omer Lavoie, interview with author, 8 October 2006.

13. Brigadier-General David Fraser, interview with author, 21 October 2006.

14. *Ibid.* "Those soldiers who criticize, they're seeing this much of the battle space," stated Fraser, holding his hands close together. "My battle space is 220,000 square kilometres. And I tell you, this is about hearts and minds. This is about winning with an idea. Our fight is not with the people of Afghanistan — they're looking at both the Taliban and their government and wondering who to side with;" Mitch Potter, "General Frets About Home Front," Middle East Bureau, 1 October 2006.

15. As quoted in Adam Day, "Operation Medusa: The Battle for Panjwai. Part I, The Charge of Charles Company," *Legion Magazine*, September/October 2007.

16. Lieutenant-Colonel Omer Lavoie, interview with author, 8 October 2006.

17. Lieutenant J. Hiltz, interview with author, 16 October 2006.

18. *Ibid.*

19. Major Matthew Sprague, interview with author, 19 November 2007.

20. One of the wounded described: "When I close my eyes, I also see the morning after Panjwayi. Sparks, smoke, fire … then the burp of the main gun of the A-10. I remember the feeling of panic as I crawled for my weapon and PPE, thinking we were under attack. I can still feel the burning on my legs and back, the shock of thinking my legs were gone. I can see the faces of the injured … the twice wounded soldiers of Charles. I see the face of the soldier who saved my life by applying tourniquets to my legs and stopping the bleeding from my back and arm." Anonymous Post, *Army.ca*, "Dealing With Being Home From Kandahar," TF 3-06 BG Notable News, 22 October 2006.

21. Brian Hutchinson, "C Company Shoulders Heavy Burden Fighting Taliban," *Times Colonist* (Victoria), 12 November 2006, A8.

22. Mitch Potter, "The Story of C Company," *Toronto Star*, 30 September 2006.

23. Captain Rob Carey, interview with author, 16 October 2006.

24. Major Greg Ivey, interview with author, 17 October 2006.

25. *Ibid.*

26. Brigadier-General David Fraser, presentation, Canadian Infantry Association Annual General Meeting, 25 May 2007.

27. The Dutch refused to provide forces for the combat component of the operation but did agree to relieve the garrison at FOB Martello so that "B" Coy could go fight. Recriminations from the RCR later surfaced that while at FOB Martello the Dutch refused to leave the compound, allowing the Taliban to regain ascendancy in the area, which the RCR had to deal with on their return.

28. Quoted in Adam Day, "Operation Medusa: The Battle For Panjwai, Part 3: The Fall of Objective Rugby," *Legion Magazine*, 26 January 2008, *www.legionmagazine.com/en/index.php/2007/11/operation-medusa-the-battle-for-panjwai-2*, accessed 8 July 2008.

29. *Ibid.*

30. *Ibid.*

31. *Ibid.*

32. *Ibid.*

33. *Ibid.*

34. *Ibid.*

35. *Ibid.*

36. Captain Piers Pappin, interview with author, 14 July 2008.

37. *Ibid.* On 5 September, "B" Coy took its first casualties (four wounded) when a group of insurgents attempted to flank their position and attacked a LAV with RPGs and recoilless rifle.

38. *Ibid.*

39. *Ibid.*

40. The unit had arrived in theatre on 22 August 2006.

41. Kenneth Finylayson and Alan D. Meyer, "Operation Medusa: Regaining Control of Afghanistan's Panjwayi Valley," *Veritas: Journal of Army Special Operations History*, Vol. 3, No. 4, 2007, 4. It must be noted that this article, with regard to the events of the Canadian Battle

Group during Operation Medusa, as well as its overall contribution, is wildly inaccurate. In addition, the dates given in the article do not correspond with the Canadian record of events.

42. *Ibid.*, 4.
43. General Rick Hillier, speech at Conference of Defence Associates Seminar, Ottawa, 15 February 2007.
44. Donald McArthur, "Canadian Troops Pressed Ahead on Operation Medusa," *Canada.com*, 6 September 2006, *www.canada.com/components/print.aspx?id+5e781f24-dd05-4e6-88c1-bbd5e09251f8&ck=50060*, accessed 16 October 2006.
45. *Ibid.*
46. Lieutenant-Colonel Shane Schreiber interview with author, 18 October 2006.
47. *Ibid.*
48. *Ibid.*

Chapter Seven

1. VCDS, NDHQ briefing, 8 May 2007. The first tanks arrived 3 October 2006.
2. Brigadier-General Dave Fraser, interview with author, 21 October 2006.
3. *Ibid.*
4. *Ibid.*
5. Commander's Entry, TF Kandahar War Diary, period 1–30 September 2006.
6. Captain Piers Pappin, interview with author, 14 July 2008.
7. Quoted in Kenneth Finylayson and Alan D. Meyer, "Operation Medusa: Regaining Control of Afghanistan's Panjwayi Valley," *Veritas: Journal of Army Special Operations History*, Vol 3, No. 4, 2007, 4.
8. Lieutenant-Colonel Shane Schreiber, interview with author, 18 October 2006.
9. *Ibid.*
10. *Ibid.*

11. Captain C. Purdy, interview with author, 17 October 2006.

12. *Ibid.*

13. Brigadier-General David Fraser, interview with author, 21 October 2006. Aside from U.S. elements of his NCE, Fraser also cut over the remnants of "C" Coy combined with Major Lussier's ISTAR Coy, as well as JTACs, FOOs, and snipers.

14. Quoted in Adam Day, "Operation Medusa: The Battle for Panjwai, Part 3: The Fall of Objective Rugby," *Legion Magazine*, 26 January 2008, *www.legionmagazine.com/en/index.php/2007/11/operation-medusa-the-battle-for-panjwai-2*, accessed 8 July 2008.

15. Lieutenant J. Bell, interview with author, 17 October 2006.

16. The Canadian troops actually developed improvised ramps to cross grape fields as an expedient method. Master-Corporal Justin O'Neil explained, "We basically took a six-foot-high I-beam, about a six-inch high I-beam, six-feet long, and then we cut six foot pickets up into about two foot sections and welded them all together and made a ramp so we could, if we had to cross any grape fields or whatnot, two or three men could lift them off the side of the LAV, lay them out, and the LAV could travel over top of them. We trialed them and there were good and bad points. We didn't actually get to employ them on Op Medusa, as we thought we might, but we have them and we've actually used them in other cases." Interview with author, 18 October 2006.

    Due to the absence of any doctrinal breaching or gap-crossing assets, Major Gasparotto, the OC of 23 Field Squadron, similarly described how the squadron "used its imagination and initiative to fabricate LAV III transportable/supportable and soldier portable ramps [that would allow] a combat loaded LAV III, weighing roughly 18 tonnes, to cross a 2.4 metre gap, which is the basic width of a small wadi." Major Mark Gasparotto, "The Road to High Readiness," in Mark Gasparotto, ed., *Clearing the Way: The Story of 23 Field Squadron in Operation Medusa and Building Route Summit*, unpublished manuscript, December 2008.

17. Commander's Entry, TF Kandahar War Diary, period 1–30 September 2006.

18. Quoted in Day, "Operation Medusa: The Battle For Panjwai, Part 3."

Major Ivey noted, "Scattered on the ground were the leaflets dropped there by NATO, warning the locals that an operation was coming through. The locals had also been warned over the radio and all the local Afghan troops knew the plan as well. This was operation was no surprise attack." Major Greg Ivey, interview with author, 17 October 2006.

19. Lieutenant-Colonel Omer Lavoie, interview with author, 8 October 2006.
20. Brigadier-General David Fraser, interview with author, 21 October 2006.
21. Major Greg Ivey, interview with author, 17 October 2006.
22. *Ibid.*
23. *Ibid.*
24. Captain C. Purdy, interview with author, 17 October 2006.
25. Major M. Wright, interview with author, October 2006.
26. Lieutenant J. Bell, interview with author, 17 October 2006.
27. Sergeant Normand Godin, interview with author, 13 October 2006.
28. Lieutenant J. Hiltz, interview with author, 16 October 2006.
29. Lieutenant J. Bell, interview with author, 17 October 2006. Sergeant Godin explained, "Most times a small door led into an open courtyard. The walls would be anywhere from 10 to 20 metres high and from one-and-a-half to two-feet thick depending on the building size. Usually you'd have your courtyards and a little living area in the corner that could probably fit a family plus. The better buildings obviously were the bigger ones. Some places you would have three or four compounds back to back." Sergeant Normand Godin, interview with author, 13 October 2006.
30. Lieutenant J. Bell, interview with author, 17 October 2006.
31. Captain Piers Pappin, interview with author, 14 July 2008.
32. Quoted in Day, "Operation Medusa: The Battle For Panjwai, Part 3."
33. Brigadier-General David Fraser, interview with author, 21 October 2006.
34. *Ibid.* On 8 September, "C" Coy, 2nd Battalion, 87th Infantry, 10th Mountain Division had arrived to reinforce TF-31. The next day they cleared the ground north of the hilltop.

35. *Ibid.*

36. *Ibid.*

37. *Ibid.*

38. Canadian Press, "Path of Little Resistance," *Kingston Whig-Standard*, 12 September 2006, 10.

39. Les Perreaux, "Afghan Battle Enters Final Phase," *Kingston-Whig Standard*, 13 September 2006, 11.

40. Brigadier-General David Fraser, interview with author, 21 October 2006.

41. *Ibid.*

42. Lieutenant-Colonel Omer Lavoie, interview with author, 10 October 2006. Lavoie noted, "Unfortunately we had very little ANA support. We were promised 300 and in the end all we received was 40. So the best I could do was push one platoon of ANA to the forward company at a time. So at any one time we had 20 ANA with the lead company to help do the clearance."

43. Quoted in Day, "Operation Medusa: The Battle For Panjwai, Part 3."

44. Brigadier-General David Fraser, interview with author, 21 October 2006.

45. Captain Piers Pappin, interview with author 14 July 2008.

46. Lieutenant J. Hiltz, interview with author, 16 October 2006.

47. Sergeant Craig Dinsmore, interview with author, 14 October 2006

48. Lieutenant-Colonel Omer Lavoie, letter to author, 25 May 2007.

49. Lieutenant-Colonel Omer Lavoie, interview with author, 10 October 2006.

Chapter Eight

1. Brigadier-General David Fraser, interview with author, 21 October 2006.

2. *Ibid.*

3. Paul Koring and Graeme Smith, "The Afghan Mission — Canadian Deaths Underscore PM's Plea to NATO," *Globe and Mail*, 28 November 2006, A1.

4. Podcast, "Audio Report by Mark Laity, NATO's civilian spokesman in Afghanistan," NATO Speeches, 22 Nov 2006, NATO Library online, *www.nato.int/docu/speech/2006/s060922b.htm*, accessed 26 November 2006.

5. NATO, Allied Command Operations, SHAPE News, "ISAF Concludes Operation Medusa in Southern Afghanistan," 17 September 2006, *www.nato.int/shape/news/206/09/060917a.htm*, accessed 24 November 2006.

6. "Operation Medusa Foiled Taliban Plans, NATO Commander Says," 20 September 2006, *london.usembassy.gov/afghn187.html*, accessed 24 November 2006.

7. NATO, "ISAF concludes Operation Medusa in Southern Afghanistan."

8. "Aid Arriving in Panjwayi Following Taliban Defeat," *ISAF News*, Issue No. 116, 1.

9. House of Commons Defence Committee, *UK Operations in Afghanistan. Thirteenth Report of Session 2006-07* (London: The Stationary Office Ltd, 18 July 2007), 16.

10. David McKeeby, "NATO's Operation Medusa Pushing Taliban from Southern Kandahar," 18 September 2006, *usinfo.state.gov/xarchives/display.html?p=washfile-english&y=2006&m=September&cx=20060 91816051idybeckcm0.9616358*, accessed 24 November 2006.

11. CTV News Staff, "Operation Medusa a 'Significant' Success: NATO," 17 September 2006, *www.ctv.ca/serviet/ArticleNews/story/CTVNews/20060917/suicid bomb 060917?sname=&noads=24Nov06*, accessed 24 November 2006.

12. Graeme Smith, "Taliban 'Eliminated' from Pivotal District," *Globe and Mail*, 18 September 2006, A14.

13. Richard Foot, "Afghanistan Sliding Into Chaos," *Montreal Gazette*, 6 Jan 2007, A3.

14. Paul Koring, "The Afghan Mission — A Thin Canadian Line Holds in Kandahar," *Globe and Mail*, 6 December 2006, A26.

15. Mitch Potter, "General Frets About Home Front," Middle East Bureau, 1 October 2006.

16. Brigadier-General Dave Fraser, interview with author, 21 October 2006.

17. Quoted in Janice Gross Stein, *The Unexpected War: Canada in Kandahar* (Toronto: Viking, 2007), 219.

18. Discussion at NDHQ, 8 May 2007.

19. CTV News Staff, "Operation Medusa a 'Significant' Success: NATO," 17 September 2006, *www.ctv.ca/serviet/ArticleNews/story/CTVNews/20060917/suicid bomb 060917?sname=&noads=24Nov06*, accessed 24 November 2006.

20. Lieutenant-Colonel Shane Schreiber, ACOS, Multi-National Brigade HQ, 1 CMBG briefing, 22 January 2007. General James Jones stated number of killed about 1,000, "but if you said 1,500 it wouldn't surprise me;" "Operation Medusa Foiled Taliban Plans, NATO Commander Says," 20 September 2006, *usinfo.state.gov/xarchives/display.html?p=washfile-english&y=2006&m=September&cx=20060920172756adtbbed0.444072*, accessed 24 November 2006.

21. Brigadier-General Dave Fraser, interview with author, 21 October 2006.

22. Major Mark Gasparotto, "Route Summit Phase 1 — Squadron Combat Team," in Mark Gasparotto, ed., *Clearing the Way: The Story of 23 Field Squadron in Operation Medusa and Building Route Summit*, unpublished manuscript, December 2008.

23. Declan Walsh, Richard Norton-Taylor, and Julian Borger, "From Soft Hats to Hard Facts in Battle to Beat Taliban," *The Guardian*, 18 November 2006, 4.

24. *Ibid.*, 5.

25. CTV News Staff, "Operation Medusa a 'Significant' Success: NATO," 17 September 2006, *www.ctv.ca/serviet/ArticleNews/story/CTVNews/20060917/suicid bomb 060917?sname=&noads=24Nov06*, accessed 24 November 2006.

26. Graeme Smith, "The Afghan Mission: Knowing the Enemy: The Taliban," *Globe and Mail*, 27 November 2006, A1.

27. Graeme Smith, "Noise of War Gives Way to the Sound of Rebuilding," *Globe and Mail*, 13 January 2007.

28. Brigadier-General Dave Fraser, interview with author, 21 October 2006.

29. Memo, Director Army Training to Commander Land Force Development Training System, "Tactical Reconnaissance Report —

Training Assessment OP Archer Rotation 3," 21 September 2006, 5.

30. Lieutenant-Colonel Omer Lavoie, interview with author, 13 October 2006.

31. *Ibid.*

32. Lieutenant-Colonel Shane Schreiber, ACOS, Multi-National Brigade HQ, 1 CMBG briefing, 22 January 2007.

33. Lieutenant-Colonel Omer Lavoie, interview with author, 13 October 2006.

34. *Ibid.*

35. Retrospectively, Lavoie assessed: "Well, I think first and foremost is the requirement to ensure at all levels that the battle, particularly for us the Canadian component, is fully thought through to the end state. And that means it must be very clear. For instance, we may have to embrace the idea of unlimited exploitation. Lines on the map look good — based on our conventional training in this case the lines looked about the right sort of amount of area that battle groups would take on. But they didn't account for the next steps forward, the terrain or type of conflict we're fighting. What we accepted as exploitation, what we all accepted and recognized as just a line on a map did not correspond to reality on the ground. The insurgents don't respect that line. So in thinking through the whole battle and, and looking beyond my own battle, which really just amounts to my areas of influence and interests, in hindsight, we should have looked beyond the doctrinal approach to exploitation." Colonel Omer Lavoie, interview with author, 13 October 2006.

36. *Ibid.*

37. Commander's Entry, Task Force Kandahar 3-06, Op Archer War Diary, 1–30 September 2006.

38. Lieutenant-Colonel Omer Lavoie, interview with author, 13 October 2006.

39. Graeme Smith, "Taliban Vow to Retake Panjwai Redoubt," *Globe and Mail*, 18 September 2006, A1.

40. Adnan R. Khan, "Prepare to Bury Your Dead," *Maclean's*, 20 March 2006, *www.macleans.ca/topstories/world/article.jsp?content= 20060320_123593_123593*, accessed 24 November 2006.

Chapter Nine

1. Interview with Lieutenant-Colonel Peter Williams, Joint Effects Coordination Officer, 22 October 2006.
2. Major Marty Lipcsey, interview with author, 20 October 2006.
3. Lavoie was awarded the Meritorious Service Medal. The commendation read in part, "LCol Lavoie through his personal courage and example led his battle group in a deliberate attack against a well entrenched enemy. Demonstrating a rare high level of professional competence and courage, LCol Lavoie created a detailed attack plan utilising coordinated fires in order to defeat the enemy and secure the objectives in the Panjwayi region." Commendation Meritorious Service Medal, Lieutenant-Colonel Omer Lavoie, 25 October 2006.
4. The "long war" refers to the counter-insurgency conflict. In a more global sense, the Americans also use the phrase to refer to the global counter-insurgency they believe themselves to be against — ideologically and religiously motivated adversaries intent on fighting the U.S., if not the entire West and its supporters, in a global jihad. Al Qaeda is prominent in this enemy grouping. The "long war" has also come to replace the term GWOT (global war on terrorism).
5. Lieutenant-Colonel Shane Schreiber, interview with author, 18 October 2006.
6. Captain Tim Button, interview with author, 9 January 2009.
7. CTV News Staff, "Operation Medusa a 'Significant' Success: NATO," 17 September 2006, *www.ctv.ca/serviet/ArticleNews/story/ CTVNews/20060917/suicid bomb 060917?sname=&noads=24Nov06,* accessed 24 November 2006.
8. Lieutenant-Colonel Shane Schreiber, ACOS, Multi-National Brigade HQ, 1 CMBG briefing, 22 January 2007.
9. Lieutenant-Colonel Omer Lavoie, interview with author, 8 October 2006.
10. It is not difficult to understand the feelings of one local Afghan who captured the sentiments of many: "We are in the middle, we aren't with the Taliban and we aren't with the government," he confessed quite frankly. "If you help us we will be with you. And if not...."

Adam Day, "The Battle for the People," *Legion Magazine*, January/February 2007, 24.

11. Elizabeth Rubin, "Taking the Fight to the Taliban," *New York Times Online*, 29 October 2006, *www.nytimes.com/2006/10/29taliban.html*, accessed 29 October 2006.

12. Montgomery Mcfate and Andrea V. Jackson, "The Object Beyond War: Counterinsurgency and the Four Tools of Political Competition," *Unrestricted Warfare Symposium 2006 Proceedings*, 150.

13. Lieutenant-Colonel Omer Lavoie, interview with author, 15 October 2006.

14. Mitch Potter, "The Story of C Company," *Toronto Star*, 30 September 2006.

15. Lieutenant-Colonel Omer Lavoie, interview with author, 15 October 2006.

16. Quoted in Declan Walsh, Richard Norton-Taylor, and Julian Borger, "From Soft Hats to Hard Facts in Battle to Beat Taliban," *The Guardian*, 18 November 2006, 5.

17. Quoted in Walsh, et al, 5. A British special operations force (SOF) officer with vast experience in the new environment asserted, "The sheer velocity of the insurgent's determination to kill us had to be gripped quickly. There was no room for error." He added, "It was kill or be killed ... It is warfare where the enemy is prepared to die to achieve his objectives. That is hard to counter and the insurgent approach has forced us to think not just out of the box, but around the corner." Michael Smith, "Secret War of the SAS," Mick Smith's Defence Blog, 18 January 2008.

18. Lieutenant-Colonel Omer Lavoie, interview with author, 15 October 2006. Work began on Route Summit on 29 September 2006; paving commenced 18 January 2007 and the project was completed 22 January 2007. Its name derived from one of the battalion's officers. The operations officer, Captain Chris French, wondered "What do we call the route?" He lived on Summit Trail in Petawawa, Ontario, so the new road quickly became Route Summit.

19. "Route Summit serves two purposes," stated Brigadier-General Tim Grant. "It's a project the local people had asked for because it will allow

commerce to flow freely in this particular area." Brian Hutchinson, "Toll for Afghan Road Paid in Soldiers' Lives," *Star Phoenix*, 12 December 2006, D7.

20. Lieutenant-Colonel Omer Lavoie, interview with author, 8 October 2006.

21. Lieutenant-Colonel Omer Lavoie, interview with author, 15 October 2006.

22. In the battle group's first two months in theatre it had suffered 15 killed and 85 wounded. With regard to the HLTA, the section leave plan was adopted from the previous tour where, under the circumstances at the time, it was found to be less disruptive and more efficient. The whole question of leave was a difficult one. No one wanted to leave their comrades short in such dangerous conditions, but the long, demanding tour made the rest very important.

23. Some ANSF were available but in inadequate numbers. Moreover, their ability, as well as their loyalties, were often suspect. The primary concern with the ANA was the fact that they had not yet arrived and their numbers were small. TF 3-06 was partnered with a Kandak from a different province and their companies numbered between 60–80 strong. Lavoie also observed that there was confusion over terms when dealing with ANA. ANA troops were actually "under operational control," Lavoie clarified, "but still, once ANA commanders are told what to do they must clear it with their Brigade commander. For example, the order to 'dig in on the road' was delayed for 1.5 days until approved by their chain of command." However, Lavoie noted that "compared to the ANP, these guys [the ANA] are Spetznaz (wear a uniform and usually don't shoot at you)." He stated that there are a number of ANP checkpoints in the battle group AOR, designed to support security through observation and physical security. But their value is questionable as Lavoie and others have walked in on checkpoints where all members have been sleeping with weapons totally accessible. According to Lavoie, most of the ANP received two weeks of training and were about 17 years old. When the ANP battalion commander arrived, Lavoie found out he was illiterate and unable to read a map. "I had to take him out

to tell/show him where to place his troops at TCPs," related Lavoie. Moreover, "ANP don't wear uniforms because they are 'uncomfortable' so there are ANP in civvies carrying AK-47 assault rifles in pickup trucks. It's hard to tell good guys from bad. For that reason there were some fratricides early on in the operation." Lieutenant-Colonel Omer Lavoie, interview with author, 13 October 2006.

24. Lieutenant-Colonel Omer Lavoie, interview with author, 15 October 2006.

25. Lieutenant-Colonel Omer Lavoie, interview with author, 13 October 2006.

26. *Ibid.*

27. Les Perreaux, "19 Day Visit to Hell," Canadian Press, TF 3-06 BG Notable News, *veritas.mil.ca/showfile.asp?Lang=E&URL=/Clips/ National/061023/f00860DN.htm*, accessed 23 October 2006.

28. Larochelle was later awarded the Military Star of Valour for his actions.

29. Quoted in Kenneth Finlayson, "Operation Baaz Tsuka, Task Force 31 Returns to the Panjwayi," *Veritas*, Vol 4, No. 1, 2008, 15.

30. "Hillier: NATO Offensive's Aim to 'Take Out' Taliban Leaders," CBC News, 15 December 2006, *www.cbc.ca/world /story/2006/12/15/ nato-offensive.html*, accessed 29 October 2007.

31. The operation was broken into four phases: The first phase was designed to shape the environment. This phase set the coordination of shuras to generate momentum towards a local security arrangement. Phase 2 was designed to interdict and dislocate the enemy. Phase 2a was designed to interdict insurgent reinforcements and exfiltration along Taliban lines of communication. Phase 2b, in turn, would disrupt the enemy by clearing and securing targeted population centres. Phase 2c was designed to secure designated areas, while Phase 2d would envelop Taliban elements in the respective zones. Phase 3 was consolidation, a combination of security, development, and information operations designed to contain the threat until the local population were able to assume a greater responsibility for their own security, thus allowing a reduction of military forces.

32. Doug Beazley, "Turning Up the Heat, Canadians Preparing for Major Role," *Toronto Sun*, 17 December 2006, 8.

33. Brian Hutchinson, "Troops Mass to Crush Taliban," *Ottawa Citizen*, 16 December 2006, A1.

34. *Ibid.*

35. Brian Hutchinson, "Troops Rallied for Falcon Summit," *National Post*, 18 December 2006, *www.canada.com/globaltv/national/story. html?id=7c3b5ffa-3b92-4f19-a075-a6076a3be794*, accessed 29 October 2007.

36. An important component of the NATO operation, particularly since the turmoil emanating from the failure of Operation Medusa to galvanize European allies to fight was the messaging that stressed "unity of effort." The latest operation stressed that "ANSF, supported by ISAF and CF are successfully accomplishing the decisive phase of the biggest ever combined operation in Southern Afghanistan." NATO themes also underlined the minimal amount of collateral damage created during the offensive.

37. Quoted in John Ferris, "Invading Afghanistan, 1836–2006: Politics and Pacification," *Calgary Papers in Military and Strategic Studies, Vol 1, Canada in Kandahar*, 19.

38. Anthony H. Cordesman, "Winning in Afghanistan: How to Face the Rising Threat," Report for the Center for Strategic and International Studies, 12 December 2006.

39. ABC News/BBC World Service Poll, "Afghanistan: Where Things Stand," 7 December 2006.

40. "Afghan Public Opinion Amidst Rising Violence," *WorldPublicOpinion. org*, 14 December 2006. A survey conducted in Afghanistan in May 2007 reported that 70 percent of Afghan males believed that the Taliban will prevail in the conflict, *CTV Nightly News*, 25 May 2007.

41. Paul Koring, "The Afghan Mission — A Thin Canadian Line Holds in Kandahar," *Globe and Mail*, 6 December 2006, A26.

42. Lieutenant-Colonel Shane Schreiber, ACOS, Multi-National Brigade HQ, 1 CMBG briefing, 22 January 2007.

43. Brooks Tigner, "Taliban Evolves to Counter ISAF," *Jane's International Defence Review*, January 2008, 4.

44. Interview with a SOF commander, Kandahar, Afghanistan, 15 March 2007.

45. Bill Graveland, "NATO Says Attack on Taliban Command Post a Message to Rebels," *The Guardian*, 15 December 2006, B8.

46. Brigadier-General David Fraser, Presentation, Canadian Infantry Association Annual General Meeting, 25 May 2007.

47. Elizabeth Rubin, "Taking the Fight to the Taliban," *New York Times Online*, 29 October 2006, *www.nytimes.com/2006/10/29taliban.htm*, accessed 29 October 2006.

48. Jeffrey Simpson, "NATO's Very Survival Hinges on the Afghan Mission," *Globe and Mail*, 29 November 2006, A29. Of note, there were only 46 suicide attacks in Afghanistan up to 22 July 2006. See also "Afghanistan's Taliban — War Without End," *The Economist*, 25 October 2007, *www.economist.com/world/asia/displaystory.cfm?story_id=10026465*, accessed 14 November 2007.

49. Anthony H. Cordesman, "Winning in Afghanistan: How to Face the Rising Threat," Report for the Center for Strategic and International Studies, 12 December 2006.

50. Brigadier-General David Fraser, interview with author, 21 October 2006.

51. Mitch Potter, "General Frets About Home Front," Middle East Bureau, 1 October 2006.

52. *Ibid.*

53. Brigadier-General David Fraser, Presentation, Canadian Infantry Association Annual General Meeting, 25 May 2007.

54. *CTV Nightly News*, 28 September 2006.

55. Michael Ignatieff, *Virtual War: Ethical Challenges* (Annapolis: United States Naval Academy, March 2001), 8.

Epilogue

1. Vincent Morelli and Paul Belkin, "NATO in Afghanistan: A Test of the Transatlantic Alliance," CRS Report for Congress, 23 January 2009,

2. The prestigious *Economist* magazine reported that "since January

[2007] almost 6,000 people have been killed, a 50% increase on last year. They included 200 NATO soldiers and more than 3,000 alleged Talibs. Insurgent violence is up by 20% on 2006," "Afghanistan's Taliban — War Without End," *The Economist*, 25 October 2007, *www. economist.com/world/asia/displaystory.cfm?story_id=10026465*, accessed 14 November 2007.

By November 2009, the coalition as a whole had lost 1,142 troops since October 2001. Dr. Liam Fox (British MP), "Beyond the Smoke: Making Progress in Afghanistan," speech to the International Institute for Strategic Studies, *www.iiss.org/recent-key-addresses/liam-fox-address*, accessed 9 October 2009.

2. "French Army Chief Rules Out Military Victory in Afghanistan," *afp.google.com/article/ALeqM5jd3DKrlYPLUzIwIfryRK7U8tAPYQ*, accessed 18 October 2008.

3. Bill Graveland, "Report: Taliban Growing Stronger," *The Chronicle Herald*, 9 December 2008, *thechronicleherald.ca/World/1094914. html*, accessed 9 December 2008. A senior officer of the Afghan Directorate of National Security professed, "This war has no tactical solution if we do not fight the Taliban at the theatre level as well and that is to attack their leadership and their headquarters where they are," A. Saleh, "Strategy of Insurgents and Terrorists in Afghanistan," Report by the Afghan National Directorate of Security, 5 May 2006.

4. *CTV News Net*, 10 March 2009.

5. General Stanley McChrystal, "ISAF Commander's Counterinsurgency Guidance," Headquarters ISAF, Kabul, Afghanistan, September 2009.

6. General Stanley McChrystal, Speech, International Institute for Strategic Studies, London, U.K., 1 October 2009.

7. *CNN Live*, 3 November 2009.

8. Bill Roggio, "Taliban Contest or Control Large Areas of Afghanistan," *www.longwarjournal.org/archives/2009/12/taliban_contest_or_c.php*, accessed 6 December 2009. In the areas under control, the Taliban operated a parallel political administration and often declared Sharia law, and ran courts, recruiting centres, and tax offices, as well as maintained security forces.

9. See, for instance, Ahmed Rashid, "How to End the War in Afghanistan," *BBC News*, *news.bbc.co.uk/2/hi/8490710.stm*, accessed 17 April 2010. Rashid noted, "There is broad agreement that talking to the Taliban is the only way to bring the insurgency to an end. No longer are the U.S., Nato or Afghanistan's neighbours talking about militarily defeating the Taliban, rebuilding the country from top to bottom or promoting democracy. Instead there is a single purpose in mind — how to provide sufficient security for development while at the same time allowing foreign forces to leave."

10. David Pugliese, "It Was the Charge of Charlie Company," *Ottawa Citizen*, 6 September 2007, A1.

11. Mitch Potter, "General Frets About Home Front," Middle East Bureau, 1 October 2006.

12. *Ibid.*

13. Canadian High Commission, "Cause for Celebration on 'Independence Day,'" *Canada Focus*, 21 September 2007, 1–2; and "NATO's Steps to an Afghan Win: Defence, Development, Diplomacy," *Globe and Mail*, 28 November 2006, A25. Importantly, the ANA desertion rate was reduced from a high 43 percent in 2006 to only 13 percent the following year with the assistance of the operational mentoring and liaison teams (OMLT). Brigadier-General David Fraser, Presentation, Canadian Infantry Association Annual General Meeting, 25 May 2007.

14. General James L. Jones and Ambassador Thomas R. Pickering, *Afghanistan Study Group Report: Revitalizing our Efforts Rethinking our Strategies* (Washington, D.C.: Center for the Study of the Presidency, 30 January 2008), 17.

15. To many, Operation Medusa actually demonstrated NATO weaknesses, particularly the myriad of national caveats. Lieutenant-Colonel Schreiber commented, "I think if you peek beneath the surface it was actually a failure for NATO because no other NATO nations showed up and nobody else wanted a piece of this," Lieutenant-Colonel Shane Schreiber, interview with author, 18 October 2006. More telling was the comment by the CDS at the time: "A year and a half ago we fought Medusa and we were there essentially alone," Interview, General Rick Hillier, CDS by Adam Day, *Legion Magazine*, 29 February 2008. Inter-

view transcript by Media Q, Inc. The fact of the matter was that despite appeals at all levels, most European allies backed away from participating. The actual combat portion of Medusa was borne by Canadians, with assistance from the Americans and a small number of ANA. The British were heavily engaged in combat operations in Helmand. No one else showed up to fight.

16. Podcast, "Audio Report by Mark Laity, NATO's Civilian Spokesman in Afghanistan," NATO Speeches 22 Nov 06, NATO Library online, *www.nato.int/docu/speech/2006/s060922b.htm*, accessed 26 November 2006.

17. Michael Tutton, "Rice Gives Nod to Military," *Kingston-Whig Standard*, 13 September 2006, 11.

18. Mike De Souza, "Focus on Our Goals, Not Our Departure," *Ottawa Citizen*, 12 September 2007, *www.canada.com/components/print. aspx?id= dfc65e-e3ab-49d3-8e4d-6490cb2945a5*, accessed 14 November 2007.

19. David McCandless, "Information Is Not Beautiful: Afghanistan," *The Guardian*, 13 November 2009, *www.guardian.co.uk/news/datablog/2009/nov/13/information-beautiful-afghanistan*, accessed 28 February 2010.

20. Canadian High Commission, "New Wave of Rebuilding in Afghanistan," *Canada Focus*, 16 February 2007, 1–2.

21. "Karzai Praises Canadian Heroes," *ISAF News*, Issue No. 116, 1.

22. Captain Tim Button, interview with author, 9 January 2009. Button also commented, "Medusa also drove the expectations of Canadian troops. Expectations were based on war stories from 1 RCR from Medusa, namely a dug in, concentrated enemy. Guys arrived looking for something to shoot. But instead, we're losing guys by covert acts of violence (i.e., IEDs) and all the technology in the world has not defeated it yet."

23. Master Warrant Officer Keith Olstad, interview with author, 11 January 2009. As of 21 January 2009, 2,700 Canadian troops were deployed at any one time, 107 had been killed, and $18.1 billion were spent in seven years of operations. Interestingly, 71 percent of Canadians said "no" to any extension of the mission in Afghanistan

and bring the troops home on schedule in 2011. Ipsos-Reid/CanWest Global, Afghanistan Mission, January 2009. DND, "Public Opinion Research," Presentation to PAPCT, 28 January 2009. A Decima-Harris poll in October 2009 indicated that 56 percent of Canadians opposed the military mission with only 36 percent in favour of it. The latest poll indicated that only 10 percent of Canadians felt the mission should be extended, 45 percent believed the "troops should stay" until 2011 when Parliament decided the Canadian military mission would end, and 41 percent wanted the troops to be pulled out early. *CTV News*, 26 October 2009.

ACKNOWLEDGEMENTS

THIS BOOK HAS BEEN in the works for far too long, however, it would have taken even longer to complete had it not been for the assistance and efforts of a multitude of people who graciously and freely gave time, thought, and effort to help me. I wish to thank all those who directly and indirectly, whether through the contribution of materials, time, a piece of their memory, or simply through their moral support, assisted me in the completion of this volume. Particularly, I wish to thank those in uniform who shared their experiences and relived the triumphs as well as the sadness that surrounds Operation Medusa.

As always, there are some who assisted more than others, and whose efforts warrant special mention. In that vein I wish to thank General (retired) Rick Hillier for his consideration in drafting the foreword and Colonel Omer Lavoie for his many candid interviews and detailed explanations of the actual battle and its aftermath. I need to acknowledge Chris Johnson for his patience and expertise in developing and continually tweaking (every time I came up with yet another modification) the detailed maps and sketches that accompany the book. I also wish to pass my gratitude to Graeme Smith who so kindly allowed me to use his dramatic photographs of the actual operation.

There are a number of others who gave generously of their time to assist with research, philosophical discussion, editorial advice, and/or proofing. I would like to thank Major Tony Balasevicius, Adam Day, Brigadier-General David Fraser, Denise Kerr, Captain Piers Pappin, and

Dr. Emily Spencer. Your efforts were greatly appreciated. I would be remiss if I did not thank Michael Carroll and Cheryl Hawley as well as the Dundurn design team for creating the polished finish product that lies before you.

Last, but certainly not least, I wish to thank my wife, Kim, and my daughters, Calli and Katie, for their continuing tolerance of my writing and historical projects.

GLOSSARY OF ABBREVIATIONS

2IC	Second-in-Command
3D	Development, Diplomacy, and Defence
ADZ	Afghan Development Zone
ALT	Air-lift Task Group
ANA	Afghan National Army
ANP	Afghan National Police
ANSF	Afghan National Security Forces
AO	Area of Operations
AOR	Area of Operational Responsibility
AQ	al Qaeda
BG	Battle Group
BHQ	Battalion Headquarters
BIP	Blow in Place
C2	Command and Control
CAS	Close Air Support
CBG	Carrier Battle Group
CCP	Casualty Collection Point
CDS	Chief of the Defence Staff
CEFCOM	Canadian Expeditionary Command
CENTCOM	Central Command

CF	Canadian Forces
CFB	Canadian Forces Base
CIDA	Canadian International Development Agency
CIMIC	Civil Military Cooperation
CINC	Commander-in-Chief
CO	Commanding Officer
Coy	Company
Coy Gp	Company Group
C/S	Call Sign
DCDS	Deputy Chief of the Defence Staff
DFAIT	Foreign Affairs and International Trade Canada
DND	Department of National Defence
EMT	Embedded Military Training [Team]
EW	Electronic Warfare
FAC	Forward Air Controller
FOB	Forward Operating Base
FOO	Forward Observation Officer
GoA	Government of Afghanistan
GMV	Ground Mobility Vehicle
GPMG	General Purpose Machine Gun
GPS	Global Positioning System
HLTA	Home Leave Travel Allowance
HMCS	Her Majesty's Canadian Ship
HQ	Headquarters
HUMINT	Human Intelligence
ICOM	Intercepted Communications
IED	Improvised Explosive Device
ISAF	International Security Assistance Force
ISR	Intelligence, Surveillance, Reconnaissance

ISTAR	Intelligence, Surveillance, Target Acquisition, Reconnaissance
JTFSWA	Joint Task Force South West Asia
JTF 2	Joint Task Force Two
KAF	Kandahar Airfield
LAV	Light Armoured Vehicle
LFCA	Land Forces Central Area
LMG	Light Machine Gun
LRPT	Long-Range Patrol Task Group
LUVW	Light Utility Vehicle Wheel
MEDEVAC	Medical Evacuation
MNB	Multinational Brigade
MND	Minister of National Defence
NATO	North Atlantic Treaty Organization
NCE	National Command Element
NCO	Non-Commissioned Officer
NGO	Non-Governmental Organization
NORAD	North American Aerospace Defense
OC	Officer Commanding
ODA	Operational Detachment Alpha
OEF	Operation Enduring Freedom
OMLT	Operational Mentoring and Liaison Team
OP	Observation Post or Operation (depending on context)
PBW	Patrol Base Wilson
PPCLI	Princess Patricia's Canadian Light Infantry
PRT	Provincial Reconstruction Team
QIP	Quick Impact Project

QRF	Quick Reaction Force
RC (S)	Regional Command (South)
RCD	Royal Canadian Dragoons
RCMP	Royal Canadian Mounted Police
RCR	Royal Canadian Regiment
Recce	Reconnaissance
RIP	Relief in Place
ROEs	Rules of Engagement
Roto	Rotation
RPG	Rocket-Propelled Grenade
SF	Special Forces
SITREP	Situation Report
SOF	Special Operations Forces
SPG	Stankovyy Protivotankovyy Granatamet (translation: anti-tank grenade launcher)
TB	Taliban
TF	Task Force
TIC	Troops in Contact
TOCA	Transfer of Command Authority
TTP	Tactics, Techniques, and Procedures
UAV	Unmanned Aerial Vehicle

INDEX

Abthorpe, Major Geoff, 87–88, 106

Afghan Development Zone (ADZ), 30, 37–38, 53, 111, 139–40

Afghan National Army (ANA), 11, 28, 51–52, 61, 72, 89, 95–96, 111, 114, 124–25, 128–29, 131, 134, 139–40, 147, 161, 164, 178, 184, 189–90

Afghan National Police (ANP), 28, 50–51, 53, 106, 111, 124–25, 161, 164, 184–85

Afghan National Security Forces (ANSF), 19, 24–25, 29, 32, 34, 49, 53–56, 111, 115, 117, 125–26, 141, 161–62, 184, 186

Afghan Transitional Authority, 20, 156

Afghanistan:

American involvement in, 17, 21, 25–26, 28, 33, 45, 49, 112

British involvement in, 145, 157, 166, 186

Canadian involvement in, 13–14, 17–18, 20–23, 24, 29, 32, 89, 92, 112, 114, 146–48, 155, 157–59, 173, 190–91

Government of, 19–24, 30–31, 35, 37, 45, 111–12, 119, 121, 138, 140–41, 153, 156, 159, 164, 189

Soviet involvement in, 41, 98, 141, 165

Taliban involvement in, 12, 19, 22, 30, 119, 146, 154, 186–87

Afghanistan Study Group, 145, 189

Aircraft

A-10 Thunderbolt, 58, 63, 77, 84–85, 88, 173

AC-130 Spectre, 38, 172

AH-64 Apache, 88, 135

B-1 Bomber, 34, 63

CP-140 Aurora Patrol Aircraft, 18

Mirage Jet, 73

UH-47 Chinook, 86, 168

Al Qaeda (AQ), 12, 16–20, 153–55, 157, 182, 195

Alexander, Chris, 23

Arghandab River, 40, 42, 59–60, 63–64, 67, 86, 93–95, 98, 106, 108, 110, 127, 171

Article 5, 16

Bayenzi, 59, 80, 107
Bazar-e-Panjwayi, 35, 50, 52–54
Bin Laden, Osama, 12, 16, 18–19,
    153–55
Blatchford, Christie, 30, 162–63, 169,
    171–72
Bonn Agreement, 19
Bules, Lieutenant Justin, 74, 76, 171
Button, Captain Tim, 122, 148, 182,
    190

Canadian Expeditionary Command
    (CEFCOM), 92, 114
Canadian International Development
    Agency (CIDA), 21
Carey, Captain Rob, 55, 75, 85, 168,
    171, 174
Carleton-Smith, Brigadier Mark, 145
Center for Strategic and International
    Studies, 142, 186–87
Central Command (CENTCOM),
    18–19, 155
Charchuk, Captain Andrew 29, 161
Chrétien, Jean, 13, 17, 154
Corby, Lieutenant Ray, 72, 131–32,
    134–38, 170
Cordesman, Anthony, 141, 186–87

Department of Foreign Affairs and
    International Trade Canada
    (DFAIT), 21
Department of National Defence
    (DND), 18, 21, 158, 191
Deputy Chief of the Defence Staff
    (DCDS), 17
Desert Eagles (see also TF-31), 89,
    138

Development, Diplomacy, and Defence
    (3D), 25
Dinsmore, Sergeant Craig, 85, 110,
    134, 178

Fawcett, Sergeant, 69–70, 72–73
Forward Operating Base (FOB)
    Martello, 25, 45, 87, 125–26, 129,
    139, 166, 174
Fraser, Brigadier-General David, 26,
    33–35, 37–40, 43–47, 49, 59–61,
    82, 86, 89–94, 97–99, 104–07,
    109, 111, 114–15, 122, 140, 142,
    146, 162–66, 173, 175–80, 187
Freakley, Major-General Benjamin,
    62, 91–92

Gauthier, Lieutenant-General Mike,
    114
Georgelin, General Jean-Louis, 145
Girouard, Chief Warrant Officer Bob,
    81, 172
Government of Afghanistan (GoA),
    13, 24–25, 29, 30–31, 35, 37, 41,
    112, 118–19, 121, 140, 158, 190
Grant, Brigadier-General Tim, 140,
    183

Hall, Major Jamie, 89–90, 96
Harper, Stephen, 23, 146
Helmand, 26, 30, 94, 113, 139, 161,
    190
Highway 1, 39–40, 53, 87–88, 90, 111,
    114, 125, 127, 129
Hillier, General Rick, 13–14, 20–21, 24,
    45, 47, 90, 93, 114, 140, 152, 156–
    57, 159, 165–67, 175, 185, 189

Hiltz, Lieutenant Jeremy, 64–65, 67, 72, 74–76, 78, 83, 102, 109, 170–71, 173, 177–78

Hope, Lieutenant-Colonel Ian, 24–29, 31–34, 38, 40, 49, 160–62

Improvised Explosive Device (IED), 28, 31, 35, 41, 65, 80, 95–96, 99, 108, 116, 121–22, 124–25, 127–29, 131, 133, 137, 163, 190

International Council on Security and Development, 145

International Crisis Group, 141

International Security Assistance Force (ISAF), 11, 13, 19–22, 26, 33, 37, 43–46, 49, 53–56, 62, 82, 91–92, 111–16, 118, 122–23, 138–40, 142, 146, 155–56, 158, 160–61, 164, 166, 179, 186, 188, 190

Ivey, Major Greg, 56–58, 63, 76–77, 85–86, 99–101, 135, 168–69, 171, 174, 177

Jackson, Warrant Officer Michael, 51–52, 167, 183

Jones, Corporal Darryl, 133, 135–37

Jones, General James L., 113, 147, 180, 189

Kabul, 13, 19–21, 30, 114, 155–56

Kandahar Airfield (KAF), 12, 46, 49, 90, 112

Kandahar City, 11, 13, 25, 29–31, 33, 35, 37, 39, 46–47, 53, 114, 118, 127, 140

Kandahar Province, 11, 13, 21–24, 27, 30–31, 116, 156, 164, 166

Karzai, Hamid, 148, 156, 190

Khalid, Assadullah, 113–14

Larochelle, Private Jesse, 132–33, 136, 185

Lavoie, Lieutenant-Colonel Omer, 49–50, 52–57, 60–61, 81–83, 86–88, 92, 94, 98–99, 107–08, 110, 116–18, 121, 123–27, 139–41, 167–69, 173, 177–78, 181–85, 193

Leakey, Captain Mike, 52

Leblanc, Master-Corporal Jeremy, 135, 137, 157

Lussier, Major Andrew, 88, 99, 104, 176

Ma'Sūm Ghar, 50–57, 59, 63–64, 72, 74–75, 77–78, 81, 84, 90, 93, 125, 129, 172

McCallum, John, 20, 156

McFarlane, Warrant Officer Ray, 128–31

Mellish, Warrant Officer Frank, 74

Mohawk 6, 98, 104, 106, 108, 112

Multi-National Brigade (MNB), 165, 180–82, 186

Nolan, Warrant Officer Rick, 67–69, 75–76

North American Aerospace Defense (NORAD), 17

North Atlantic Council, 16, 154

North Atlantic Treaty Organization (NATO), 11–13, 16, 20, 22–24, 26–27, 31, 35, 41, 44–47, 49, 62, 81, 87, 90–92, 97, 106, 112–16, 121–23, 125–26, 138–39, 146–48,

151–52, 154, 156, 158, 163–66,
177–80, 182, 185–90
Northern Alliance, 19

Objective Cricket, 104, 106
Objective Rugby, 58–59, 61–62, 65,
79–80, 92, 96, 98, 104, 106, 108,
110–11, 121, 174, 176
O'Connor, Gordon, 22, 157
Operation Apollo, 17, 155
Operation Archer, 22, 24
Operation Athena, 20–21
Operation Baaz Tsuka, 39–40, 185
Operation Enduring Freedom (OEF),
12, 17, 29, 160
Operation Medusa, 176–80, 182, 186,
189
Operation Mountain Thrust, 27
Ottawa, 44, 92, 157

Pakistan, 30, 40, 94, 139
Panjwayi, 11, 15, 26, 29–32, 35, 38–39,
53–55, 59, 81, 106, 111, 115, 122,
128, 138–40, 173, 182
Pappin, Captain Piers, 89, 95, 104, 109,
174–75, 177–78
Parsons, Master-Corporal Matthew,
32, 162
Pashmul, 13, 27, 29, 31, 35, 37–39,
42–44, 46, 49, 53–56, 78, 82–83,
85, 89, 92, 95–98, 104, 110–12,
118–19, 125, 138, 167
Patrol Base Wilson (PBW), 52, 87,
124, 129, 131, 137, 139
Princess Patricia's Canadian Light
Infantry (PPCLI):
1st Battalion (1 PPCLI), 24, 26,

28, 29, 159, 162, 166–67
"A" Coy, 50
"C" Coy, 29
2nd Battalion (2 PPCLI), 129
3rd Battalion (3 PPCLI), 20, 155
Provincial Reconstruction Team (PRT),
13, 21, 25, 131, 156–57, 160
Purdy, Captain Chris, 38, 42–43, 80–
81, 97, 101, 164–65, 172, 176–77

Regional Headquarters (South)
(RC[S]), 138
Registan Desert, 90, 94, 97, 139
Rice, Condoleezza, 148, 190
Richards, Lieutenant-General David,
35, 44–45, 62, 91–92, 113–14
Route Summit, 125, 127, 140, 176,
180, 183
Royal Canadian Dragoons (RCD), 88
Royal Canadian Mounted Police
(RCMP), 21
Royal Canadian Regiment (RCR):
1st Battalion (1 RCR), 11, 15, 49,
50, 62, 71, 90, 94, 96, 98, 106,
112, 121, 126, 140, 167, 190
"A" Coy, 50–52, 54, 101,
106, 108
"B" Coy, 87–89, 93,
95–96, 98, 101, 104,
106, 108, 174
"C" Coy (Charles Coy),
54–55, 59, 62–65,
67–68, 71–73, 76–
78, 83, 85–86, 90, 93,
106, 109, 110, 132,
137, 176
ISTAR Coy, 104, 176

Rubin, Barnett, 114
Rules of Engagement (ROEs), 117, 130

Scheffer, General Jaap de Hoop, 44, 91
Schreiber, Lieutenant-Colonel Shane, 27, 30–31, 39–41, 47, 61–62, 78, 91–92, 97, 115, 117, 122–23, 142, 161–62, 164–67, 169, 171, 175, 180–82, 186, 189
Senlis Council, 29, 145, 161
Siah Choy, 94, 96, 106–07, 117, 167
Special Operations Forces (SOF), 12, 19–20, 33, 74–75, 94, 97, 155, 168, 172, 183, 187
Sperwan Ghar, 94, 96, 104, 106–07
Sprague, Major Matthew, 54–55, 59–61, 63–65, 73–74, 76–78, 84, 168–71, 173
Standing Committee on National Security and Defence, 17
Strong Point Centre, 129, 131–32, 135, 137–38

Taliban, 11–13, 17–20, 22, 26–35, 37–44, 46–47, 49–59, 62, 64–65, 72, 76, 78, 80, 82–83, 85, 87, 90, 92–94, 96–101, 103–07, 109–19, 121–31, 133, 137–42, 146–48, 153–54, 157, 160, 162–65, 172–74, 179–83, 185–89
Task Force (TF) 3-06, 38, 49–50, 53, 82, 94–95, 98, 104, 106–07, 109, 111, 121, 123, 126–27, 137, 167, 173, 181, 184–85
Task Force (TF) 31, 89–90, 94, 96–97, 104–05, 107, 177

Task Force (TF) Grizzly, 93–94, 97, 104–07, 109
Task (TF) Kandahar (*see also* TF 3-06 and 1 RCR), 53–54, 168, 175–76
Task Force (TF) Orion, 24–29, 32, 34, 38, 49, 59, 80, 160–61, 163, 171
Teal, Corporal Sean, 68, 70, 170
Towers, Sergeant Patrick, 33, 162

United Nations (UN), 16–17, 152–53, 156, 158–59
United Nations Security Council Resolution (UNSCR), 13, 19, 153–56
Unmanned Aerial Vehicle (UAV), 55, 159, 168
Uruzgan, 26, 30, 113, 139, 166

Van Loon, Major-General Ton, 139–40

Walsh, Sergeant Jamie, 75, 132, 134, 136, 171, 180, 183
Wessan, Captain Derek, 65, 70, 109
Williams, Lieutenant-Colonel Peter, 38, 121–22, 164, 182
Williams, Lieutenant-Colonel Steve, 97–98
World Trade Center, 12, 15
Wright, Major Mike, 50–53, 101, 167, 177

Zhari, 29–30, 111–12, 114, 138–40, 147

11 September 2001 (9/11), 12, 15, 106, 152

By the Same Author

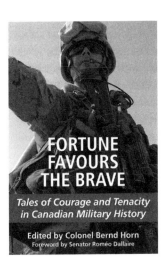

Fortune Favours the Brave
Tales of Courage and Tenacity in
Canadian Military History
Colonel Bernd Horn, ed.
978-1-55002-816-4
$35.00

Many Canadians see the role their country's military plays in Afghanistan as an anomaly. However, this assumption is far from the truth. As U.S. Secretary of State Condoleezza Rice has commented, "Canadians are fierce fighters." *Fortune Favours the Brave* certainly proves this point in a collection of essays that showcases the fighting spirit and courage of Canada's military.

Daring actions featured in the book include the intrepid assault on the Fortress of Louisbourg and the cat-and-mouse struggle between Canadian partisans and Rogers's Rangers in the Seven Years' War in the 1750s; the seesaw battle for the Niagara frontier in the War of 1812; an innovative trench raid in the First World War; the valiant parachute assault to penetrate the Third Reich in the Second World War; the infamous battle at Kap'yong in the Korean War; covert submarine operations during the Cold War; the Medak Pocket clash in Croatia in the early 1990s; and Operation Medusa in Afghanistan.

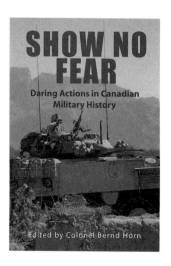

Show No Fear
Daring Actions in Canadian Military History
Colonel Bernd Horn, ed.
978-1- 55002-841-6
$35.00

Show No Fear is a collection of essays that captures the richness of Canadian military history. Although Canadians see their nation as a peaceable kingdom and themselves as an unmilitary people, the truth is that Canada has a proud military heritage. Moreover, the nation's citizens and their descendants share a legacy of courage, tenacity, and warfighting prowess. This volume of daring actions showcases the country's rich and distinct national military experience while capturing the indomitable spirit of the Canadian soldier.

Actions studied include military bravery in the Seven Years' War, the British attacks on Fort Mackinac and Fort Detroit in the War of 1812, the Lake Erie expeditions during the American Civil War, courage displayed at Paardeberg in the Boer War, trench raiding in the First World War, bold valour in the ill-fated Dieppe Raid in the Second World War, toe-to-toe fighting with the Chinese in the Korean War, and present-day heroics in Afghanistan.

Available at your favourite bookseller.

DUNDURN PRESS
www.dundurn.com

What did you think of this book?
Visit www.dundurn.com
for reviews, videos, updates, and more!